GREEN BELT
KENKEN®
300 PUZZLES

CREATED BY
TETSUYA MIYAMOTO

PUZZLE
WRIGHT
PRESS

New York

CONTENTS

Introduction

3

Puzzles

5

Answers

155

PUZZLE
WRIGHT
PRESS
New York

An Imprint of Sterling Publishing
387 Park Avenue South
New York, NY 10016

ISBN 978-1-4549-0418-2

Distributed in Canada by Sterling Publishing
C/o Canadian Manda Group, 165 Dufferin Street
Toronto, Ontario, Canada M6K 3H6
Distributed in the United Kingdom by GMC Distribution Services
Castle Place, 166 High Street, Lewes, East Sussex, England BN7 1XU
Distributed in Australia by Capricorn Link (Australia) Pty. Ltd.
P.O. Box 704, Windsor, NSW 2756, Australia

For information about custom editions, special sales, and premium and
corporate purchases, please contact Sterling Special Sales at 800-805-5489 or
specialsales@sterlingpublishing.com.

Manufactured in Canada

10

www.puzzlewright.com

INTRODUCTION

KenKen is a fairly new puzzle. It was invented in 2004 by Tetsuya Miyamoto, a math teacher from Yokohama, Japan, as a tool to help improve his students' math and logic skills. He wanted something that would be entertaining enough to keep students interested, and, as it happened, he succeeded extremely well in creating something entertaining—people all over the world now solve and enjoy his invention daily.

KenKen, at first glance, may look a bit like sudoku. And, like sudoku, the rows and columns of a KenKen grid contain no repeated numbers. But that's where the similarities end. Here are the basic rules of KenKen:

- Fill the grid so that each row and column contains a complete set of digits, with no repeated digits in any row or column. (The set of numbers depends on the size of the grid; a 4×4 KenKen puzzle will use the numbers from 1 to 4, a 5×5 KenKen puzzle will use the numbers from 1 to 5, and so on.)
- Each heavily outlined box, known as a "cage," indicates a mathematical operation that must match the digits inside that cage. Numbers may repeat within a cage as long as they do not appear in the same row or column.

There are four mathematical operations that may appear in a KenKen puzzle. A plus sign indicates that the digits inside the cage add up to the given number, while a multiplication sign indicates that the given number is the product of the digits inside the cage. If a cage contains a minus sign, the given number is the difference between the digits in the cage (that is, the result of subtracting the smaller digit from the larger digit). In a cage with a division sign, the given number is the quotient of the digits in the cage (that is, the result of dividing the larger digit by the smaller digit). Cages with minus signs and division signs will never contain more than two digits. Single-cell cages contain no mathematical symbols, and simply indicate what digit they contain.

Now that you know the basics, let's turn the page and take a look at a sample puzzle, and solve it together.

First, we can fill in any 1×1 cages right away. There's one on the right side of the grid, and we can write a 1 in it. Below that is a rectangular cage with a quotient of 2. Since this is a 4×4 puzzle, which only uses the digits 1 through 4, that cage can only contain either the digits 1 and 2 ($2 \div 1 = 2$), or 2 and 4 ($4 \div 2 = 2$). Since that column already has a 1 in it, the correct pair must be 2 and 4, but we don't yet know which order they go in, so let's look elsewhere for more information. The 6+ clue on the bottom of the grid is helpful, because that's the lowest possible sum of three different digits ($1 + 2 + 3 = 6$); that means that cage must contain 1, 2, and 3. That accounts for three of the four digits in the row, so the remaining digit is a 4—which means we can now write the 2 in the other space of the 2÷ cage.

Other good places to look for information are in cages with high given numbers, which usually have fewer possible solutions. Take a look at the 16× cage. There are only two ways to make that product: $1 \times 4 \times 4 = 16$, or $2 \times 2 \times 4 = 16$. (In a larger puzzle, $1 \times 2 \times 8$ might be possible, but this grid contains no digits higher than 4.) Both of those solutions contain a pair of repeated digits, which must go in the two diagonally adjacent corners of that cage, so they don't share a row or column. But they can't both be 2's, since the third row already has a 2 in it, so they must be 4's, making the remaining cell in that cage a 1. And now the third row contains every digit but 3, so we can write that into the empty cell.

Whenever you write a digit in an empty cage, see if that new data helps solve that cage. In this case, we've just written a 3 into a 1− cage. That cage's digits must have a difference of 1, so they could be 2 and 3 ($3 - 2 = 1$) or 3 and 4 ($4 - 3 = 1$). But the second row already contains a 4, so the digit above the 3 must be 2. In fact, now that all but one 4 has been placed, only one possible square remains for the last 4, at the top of the third column. With that 4 written in, you should be able to easily complete that cage (and the rest of the puzzle). The solution appears upside-down at right.

Remember, every KenKen can be solved logically; you never need to guess to complete a puzzle. This book contains 300 medium puzzles: 90 5×5 KenKen, 180 6×6 KenKen, and 30 7×7 KenKen. Difficulty will increase gradually as you go. Happy solving!

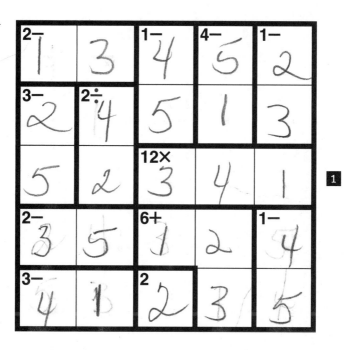

1

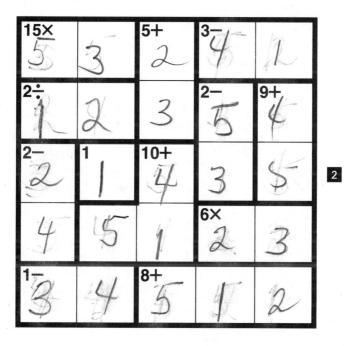

2

5

4+ 1	4− 5	3 3	2÷ 2	4
3	4	1− 4	5	3− 2
120× 4	3	1− 2	1	5
5	2	4− 4	1− 4	2− 3
2÷ 2	4	5	3	1

20
6

6+ 2	6+ 5	2− 3	1	2÷ 4
3	1	1− 4	5	2
1	2÷ 4	2	9+ 3	15× 5
20× 5	2÷ 2	1	4	3
4	2− 3	5	2	1

234   24

Puzzle 5

5+ 1	4	1− 2	9+ 5	2− 3
2÷ 2	1	3	4	5
60× 3	3− 2	5	3− 1	4
4	4− 5	1	1− 3	2
5	1− 3	4	2÷ 2	1

5

Puzzle 6

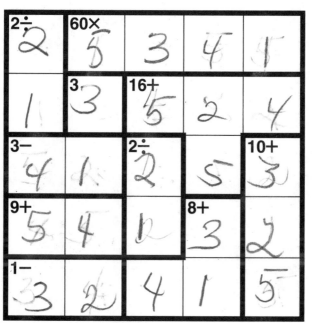

2÷ 2	60× 5	3	4	5
1	3	16+ 5	2	4
3− 4	1	2÷ 2	5	10+ 3
9+ 5	4	1	8+ 3	2
1− 3	2	4	1	5

6

4
3
5
1
2
5

Puzzle 7 (5×5):

2÷ 2	1	24× 4	3	5 5
4 4	12+ 5	2	6+ 1	3
6+ 1	4	2− 3	5	2
5	3	8× 1	2	4
30× 3	2	5	3− 4	4

Puzzle 8 (5×5):

40× 2	5	4	5+ 1	3
1− 4	3+ 2	2− 5	3	1
5	1	1− 3	2	11+ 4
12× 3	4	4− 1	5	2
2− 1	3	2÷ 2	4	5

Puzzle 9

11+ 2	4	6× 3	4− 5	1
5	2÷ 1	2	10+ 3	4
2− 1	2	9+ 5	5+ 4	3
3	13+ 5	4	1	9+ 2
4	3	1	2	5

Puzzle 10

9+ 4	1− 3	10× 2	5	1
5	2	3− 4	1	30× 3
2− 3	5+ 4	1	2÷ 2	5
1	5− 5	12+ 3	4	2
2÷ 2	1	5	1− 3	4

1− 5	2÷ 1	2	1 3	4
4	1− 3	2	1− 5	10× 2
6+ 1	2	3	4	5
2− 3	4	6+ 4	1	2
1− 4	5	1	6× 2	3

6+	40×		6+	
	2−		2÷	
		8+	15×	
1−	8+			1−
			4 4	

Puzzle 1/3 (5×5 grid):

2÷		2−		60×
8+	10+	5	1−	
	15×		6+	
5		2−		

Puzzle 1/4 (5×5 grid):

10+		1−		24×
	2÷		4−	
1−	2−			
	20×		2÷	
6×			1−	

Puzzle 1 (5×5):

2−		5	4−	1−
6+	2÷			
	1−	1−		1
		2−	10×	
2−			2−	

Puzzle 2 (5×5):

60×			2÷	5
	8+	2−		5+
			7+	
3−	2−	1−		1−
			5	

Puzzle 1/7

2÷	11+	20×		
			8+	1−
14+		5+		
	8×			2
			2−	

7

Puzzle 1/8

2−	2÷	2−	2−	
			4−	1−
24×		10+		
			1−	4+
1−		2		

1
8

3

Puzzle 19

4+	2÷	1−		2÷
		60×		
2−		8×		
40×				2−
	6+			

Puzzle 20

7+	1−	2	15×	
		4+	1−	
	2÷			40×
2−		8+		
	1−			

14

Puzzle 2-1

12+			36×	
2÷	30×			
			1−	
2−	1−		2	10×
	3−			

Puzzle 2-2

20×	8+		2−	
		9+		
6+		1−		2÷
24×		7+		
	1−			5

8×			2−	
8+	2−	3−		4
		2÷		6+
2÷	1−	3−		
		2−		

10×		2÷	8+	
	1−		3−	
1−		45×		1−
1−		10+		

16

2÷		4+	2−	
2−	20×		2−	
		20×	8+	
2÷				1−
2−		1−		

1−	48×	5	2÷	
			4−	
2÷			11+	
12+	6+			1−
		2÷		

Puzzle 2/7 (6×6 grid)

2−		2÷		1−	
2÷	6×				
	1−	10+			
6+		30×	2÷		
			1−		

Puzzle 2/8 (6×6 grid)

2÷		12×	4−	3−	
10+					
		40×	8+		
2−					
10×			1−		

1−		20×		8+
5+				
2÷	15×		3	40×
	4			
5	1−		1−	

40×	2−		2÷	
		4−		2−
1−	8+	20×		
		1−		3−
1−		1−		

3 / 1

6+			1−	
3−	12×	1−	2÷	
			2−	
12×		10×	2−	2÷

3 / 2

1−		120×	2÷	
5+			15×	
2			1−	
6+				1−
2−		3−		

Puzzle 1

3−	10×	1−		1−
		10+		
2−				4−
1−	3−	2÷	60×	

Puzzle 2

20×			8+	
3−		10×	2−	
	2−			40×
2−		2÷		
	1−			

Puzzle (top)

6+	120×			
		11+	3−	
4			2−	2÷
2−	2÷	2÷		
			1−	

Puzzle (bottom)

1−		5	2÷	
6+	2÷		30×	
	6+		13+	
				7+
1−		1−		

2÷	75×	2÷		12+
			2÷	
9+	5+			
		2−	8+	2÷
1−				

3−		15×	8+	3−
1−				
2−	7+			2
		2÷	1−	
3−			8+	

Puzzle 39

20×	4−		2−	1−
	2−			
	2	12+		
10+	8+		4−	
			2÷	

Puzzle 40

13+	24×			2÷
	1−		2÷	
		11+		60×
2−				
	1		2−	

4 1

2−		75×	8+	
10+	1−			4
				10+
	2−			
2÷		1−		

4 2

3−	60×	4−		4
		9+		2−
1−				
	9+		1−	
2÷			1−	

25

Puzzle 4/3:

30×	40×		1	10+
	1−		1−	
	2−		13+	2÷
5+				

Puzzle 4/4:

1−		12×		10×
9+				
1−		9+		2÷
8+	1	2÷		
			2−	

Puzzle 4/5

3−		12+		
4−	2÷	5	12×	
				8+
1−	2−	9+		
		2÷		

Puzzle 4/6

1−		2÷		15×
1−		1−		
1	2−		12+	
3−		4−		
2−			2÷	

4/7

20×	2−		2÷	
	7+		15×	
		1−		12×
1−	3−		4−	
	1−			

4/8

2÷		3	4−	
10×	1−		9+	2÷
	10+			
4+			2÷	
	11+			3

49

30×			5+	
1−	6+	2−		60×
2÷	10×			12×
	1−			

50

10×	30×		11+	
	1			2÷
	24×	20×		
1−			8+	2−

2−	3−		3−	
	1−		40×	4+
3−	3			
	2−		2÷	
2−		9+		

2−		40×		
2	9+			5+
12+	2÷	20×		
			2−	5+
	2÷			

4−	2−	1−		8×
		5+		
2÷		11+		
4			11+	8+
2−				

2÷		2−		8×
1−		4+		
30×			4	
1−	3−		7+	
	1−		2−	

30×	8+		1−	
		2÷		6+
	4−	1−	9+	
3−				
	1−			5

24×		12+	1−	
				2−
1−	20×			
	20×	2−	3−	
			2÷	

Puzzle 5/7

2−		40×		8×
5+			2−	
1−	9+	1		
		1−	2÷	2−
5				

Puzzle 5/8

2÷		13+	12×	
1−				
10+	8+		5+	6×
	1−			
	2−		5	

33

Puzzle 1 (5×5 KenKen):

15×	8+	7+		
			1−	
	10+		10×	
2÷				1−
9+		4+		

Puzzle 2 (5×5 KenKen):

3−	40×			9+
	15×	1−		
			2÷	
1−	1−	1−		5+
		15×		

Puzzle 6 / 1

6×	6+		2÷	
	7+		10+	2−
	2	5+		
1−	2−			1−
		1−		

Puzzle 6 / 2

10×	2÷		2−	
	5+		1−	1−
	4−			
1−		9+		9+
3−				

Puzzle 1 (top):

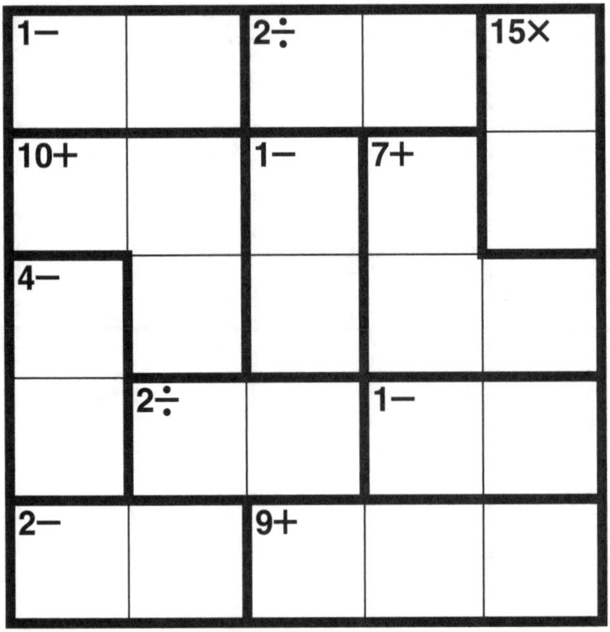 1−		2÷		15×
10+		1−	7+	
4−				
	2÷		1−	
2−		9+		

Puzzle 2 (bottom):

12+	12×			2÷
		5	6+	
	8+			
1−		2÷	15+	
5+				

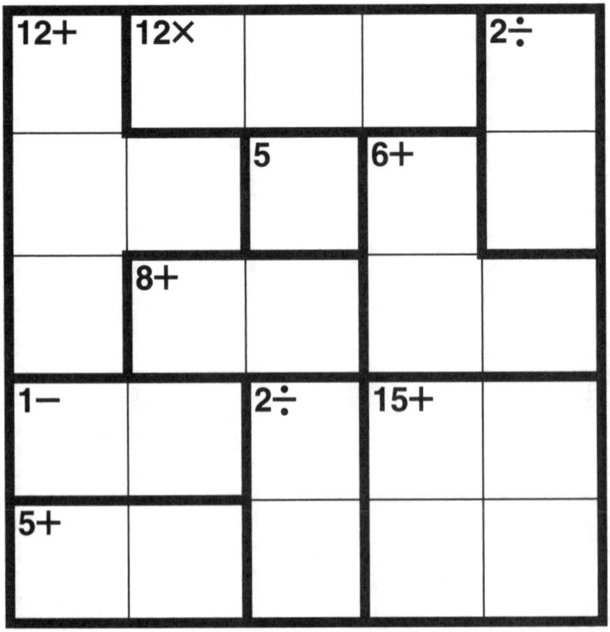

11+		15×		
	9+	13+	2÷	
2				1−
2−			30×	
	5+			

30×			2÷	1−
2−	9+			
	1−	3−	6+	
9+			2−	
	1−		2−	

6/7

2−	1−		2÷	
	1−	1−		20×
5		2÷		
2÷	9+		1−	
			1−	

6/8

12×		9+	3−	
6+				1−
		2÷		
3−		2÷	11+	
1−				

4−		1−		3−
6×		1−		
7+	2−	2÷		3−
		1−		
	1−		2−	

2÷		20×		9+
4−		1−		
14+			2−	
	2−		20×	
	1−			2

Puzzle 7-1

8+	2÷		11+	
	15×			
	60×	2	20×	7+
3−				
		6+		

Puzzle 7-2

100×		2−		2÷
	1−	2−		
2÷		14+		
	2−			1−
1−		4−		

Puzzle 1 (top)

6×		3−		10+
1−		1−		
	60×		2÷	
1−	60×			30×

Puzzle 2 (bottom)

1−	2−	2÷		5
		40×	2−	1−
3−				
2−	2÷		4	8+
		3		

7
5

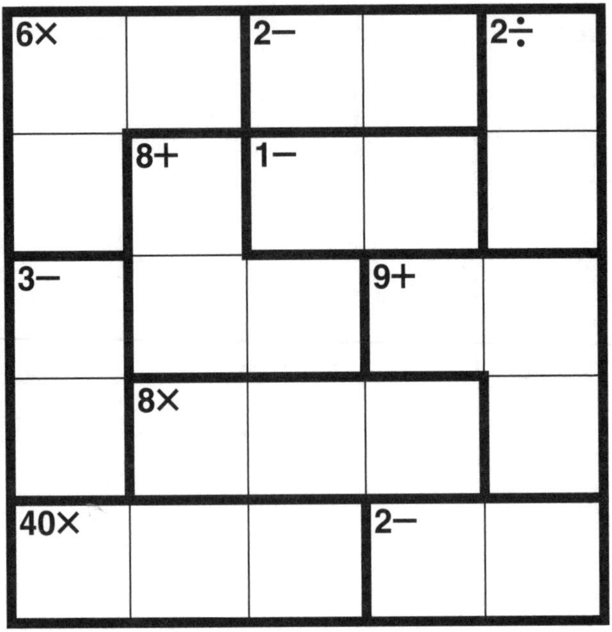
6×
2−
2÷
8+
1−
3−
9+
8×
40×
2−

7
6

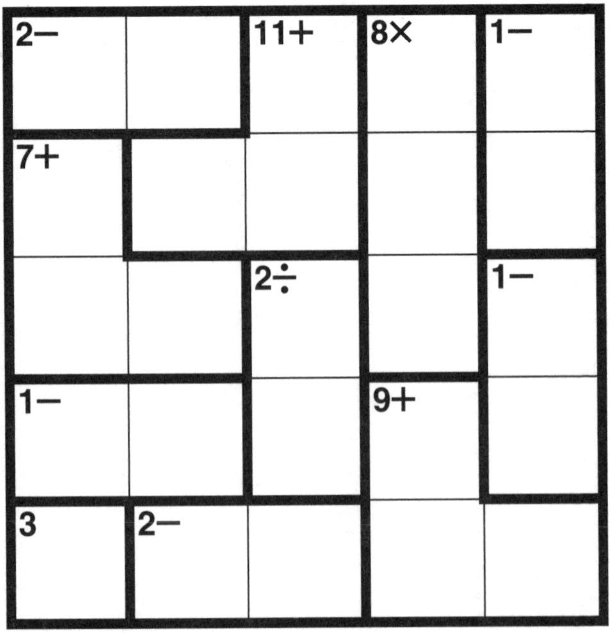
2−
11+
8×
1−
7+
2÷
1−
1−
9+
3
2−

Puzzle 7/7

40×		11+	1−	
3			5+	
2÷	12×			2−
			2−	
8+				4

Puzzle 7/8

96×		4−		8+
2−		1−		
			40×	
12+	2÷			1−
		2−		

Puzzle 79

11+	1−		2−	
	1−	12×		8+
		20×		
2−	4−	1−		
			2÷	

Puzzle 80

2÷	4+		1−	
	1−	1−	2	5+
1−			2−	
	3−			1−
2−		20×		

8
1

8
2

Puzzle 1 (5×5):

7+	60×		3−	
		1−		2−
	2	10×		
2−	10+		12×	2÷

Puzzle 2 (5×5):

60×	4−		7+	1−
	10+			
			3−	
2÷	2−		1	20×
	4	1−		

1−	2÷	6×		4−
			8+	
3−				10+
2−	1−			
	6+		2−	

3−	2−	8×		1−
			4+	
1−		3		1−
2−	2	1−		
	1−		2÷	

8
7

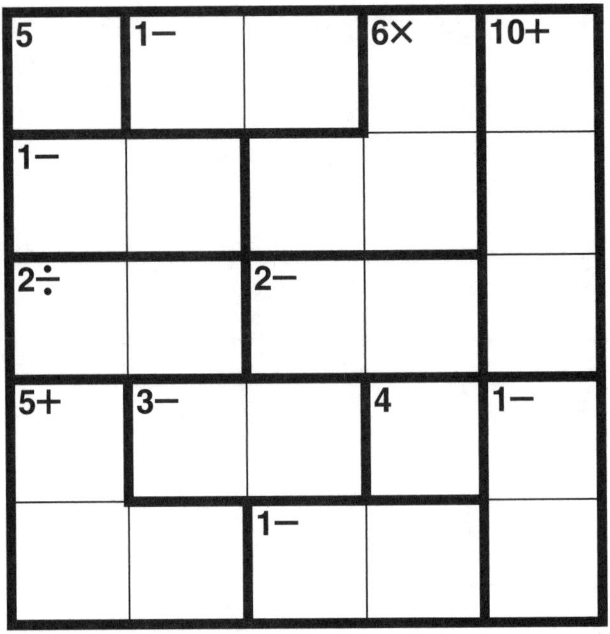

8
8

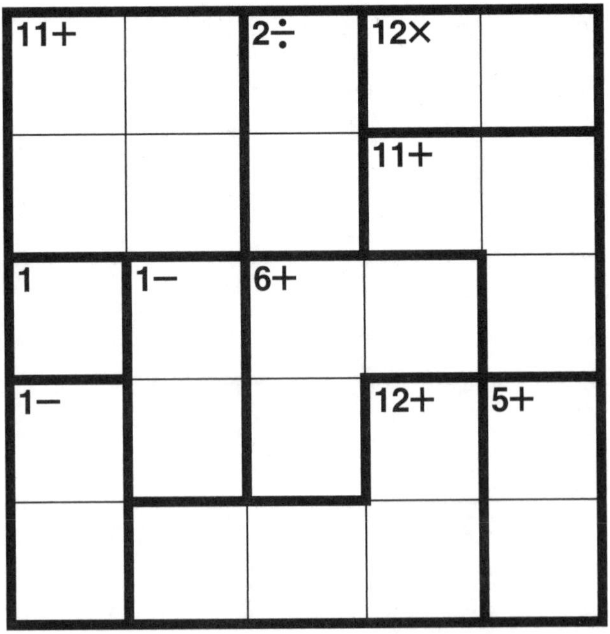

Puzzle 8/9

20×		3−		1−
2÷		7+		
	12+	12+		
			1−	10×

Puzzle 9/0

2−		6+		15×
2÷	60×			
		6+	2−	
2−			24×	5
1−				

9/1

3	3+		1−	2−	
8×		2−		3÷	3÷
3−			6		
	5−		2−		40×
2÷		2−		3÷	
1−		5−			

9/2

2−		2÷	90×		
1−	11+			5−	5
		3−			3+
2÷	72×			90×	
	10×				2−
5		9+			

93

1−		3÷	20×		12+
11+			3+		
8×		11+	2−		
5−			5+		3
	12+	2÷	3−	3÷	6+

94

5	180×		5−		10+
3−			2÷	1−	
	5−	40×			
2÷				2−	
	8+	4−	30×		4−
			5+		

3−	3÷		2−	10×	
	2÷	3÷		2÷	1−
2÷			11+		
	40×			9×	
		13+	5−		
			1−		6

15×	2÷		7+	3−	
	15+			5−	5+
	10×		2÷		
12+		5−		1−	3
	3÷		1		3−
		3	2−		

Puzzle 9/7

10+	30×		3÷	3÷	
	80×			1−	
		4+		3÷	
8+	3÷	5+		11+	9+
		5−	80×		
1−					

Puzzle 9/8

6×	20×			1−	
	2÷		1−		2−
2÷	3+	2÷		15×	
		5−			11+
13+		10+	2		
3				5−	

53

72×			3÷	3−	3÷
4	15×				
2−		11+	2−	3−	
	3+			5−	
12×		24×		11+	
		7+		4	

5	1−		12×	5−	
20×				5+	
2÷	2÷		1−		8+
	10+		3÷		
3+			1−		6
3÷		15×		5+	

101

4	5−	2−	30×		
3+			4−		2÷
	1−	1−		10×	
2÷		5−			2÷
	3	15×	5+		
3−			4	5−	

102

600×	3÷		5−	2÷	
		9+		5−	1−
			72×		
2÷	6			8+	4−
	5+	15+			
3				3÷	

103

5+	60×			3÷	
	5−		6×		15×
1−		13+		5−	
2÷	2				2÷
	3−		8+	10+	
6×		6			

104

5	2÷		2÷		24×
48×	11+		3−		
	3−			20×	18×
	2÷		3−		
7+		15+			
				3−	

Puzzle 105 (6×6):

2−	2÷	11+	180×		2×
2−	2÷			3−	
	1−	5−		2÷	9+
2÷		3÷			
	24×			30×	

Puzzle 106 (6×6):

1−		4−		3÷	
4−		1−		3÷	
3−		9+	3+		72×
3+			2−		
13+		10×		10+	
	2	5−			

Puzzle 107

2÷		5	18×		
3÷	90×	2÷		4−	
			3−	1−	11+
1−	8×				
		90×		2÷	
6+				2−	

Puzzle 108

16+		12×			3÷
	12×		3+	7+	
3−					5+
7+		11+		12+	
	2÷	16+			
4				2÷	

3−		1−	6+	3÷	12×
1−	24×				
		14+	7+		
3÷				6	20×
	3+		10+		
4−		3−		2−	

100×		10+	18×		6+
5−				15+	
	1−				
144×	2−		3÷		9+
		15×			
	10×		1	2−	

1 1 1

2−	2÷		10×		
	2−	10+		3÷	
5		8×		2−	
3÷			30×		14+
	3+		96×		
10+				1	

1 1 2

10×	3+		2÷		1−
	10+	3−	6×		
1−			150×	5+	
	9+	12×		5−	
5−					20×
		2−			

Puzzle 113

5−		15×	11+	32×	
8×	7+			3	
		3−		1−	3÷
	3÷		36×		
60×				30×	
	1−		3+		

Puzzle 114

5−		24×			11+
3÷	10+	6+	5+		
			11+	6+	
3−	9+				6
		2÷	10+		3÷
9+			2÷		

Puzzle 115

3÷	5−		60×		
	8+			3	10+
1−		2÷	11+		
6+	3÷			4−	
		2÷	24×		1−
9+			3+		

Puzzle 116

3−		3÷		24×	
72×			4−		10×
3−		2÷		8+	
12×	2−				1
	2÷		11+		2÷
	6+		1−		

Puzzle 117

3−		2−		1−	6
2÷	24×		3+		7+
	3	1−		6×	
2÷			1−		8+
20×	5−	2		1−	
		11+			

Puzzle 118

12×			11+		3−
15×	5−	32×	6×		
					2÷
10+	11+		3−		
		6+	3−	1−	
7+				2÷	

20×	3−	6×	11+		2÷
			10+		
15×		5−			9+
6	2÷	1−	5+		
1−				10+	2÷
	20×				

11+	3÷	12×		40×	
			3÷		
1−		60×			4−
2÷	5−		3−	12×	
	3÷				2÷
8+			24×		

Puzzle 1:

3	4−		48×		
12+			5−		3+
36×			30×	3−	
11+	5+	2÷			2÷
				13+	
3+		2−			

1
2
1

Puzzle 2:

5−		20×		6×	7+
3−	11+				
	8+			30×	2
1−	5+				5−
	2−		11+		
1	2÷		11+		

1
2
2

65

Puzzle 1 (1 2 3):

2÷	72×		3÷	3−	5−
	5				
16+			36×		
1−			3−		2−
5−	3+		3−	96×	
	2−				

Puzzle 2 (1 2 4):

3+		30×		12×	
24×		10×	1−		3÷
1−			10+		
	1−	9+	5−		13+
6×			40×		
	3				

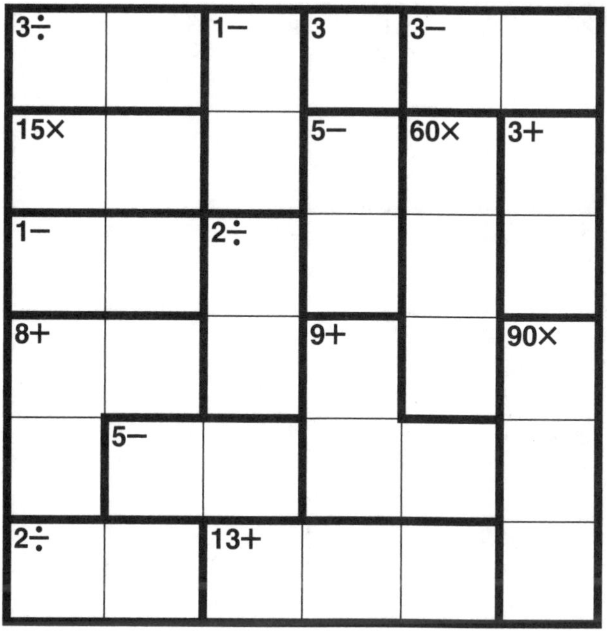
3÷
1−
3
3−
15×
5−
60×
3+
1−
2÷
8+
9+
90×
5−
2÷
13+

1
2
5

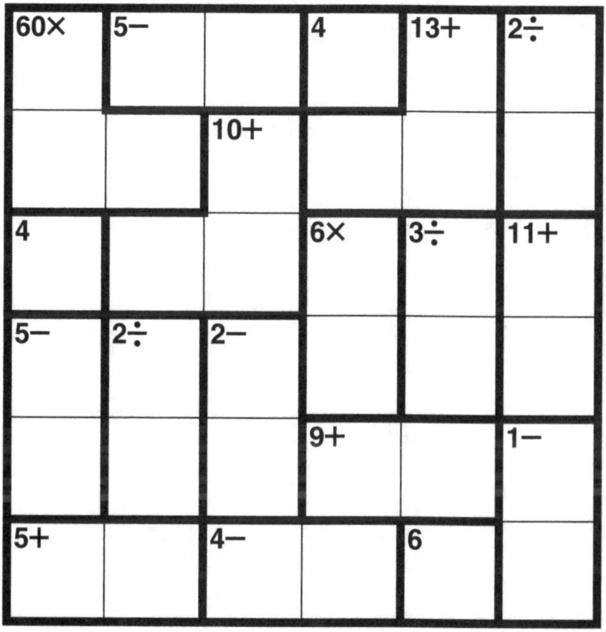
60×
5−
4
13+
2÷
10+
4
6×
3÷
11+
5−
2÷
2−
9+
1−
5+
4−
6

1
2
6

Puzzle 127

24×	6	3−	4−	3−	
				8+	
5−	8+		2÷		
	2÷	9+		1−	
20×			1−		2÷
	6+		3÷		

Puzzle 128

2÷	1−	1−		5−	
		1−	4−		12×
12+	6×		4	2÷	
		3+			
	5−	7+	30×	2÷	
3				10×	

1−	600×	5−		3÷	2÷
			2		
11+		36×	3+		6
	2÷		12×		14+
1−			120×		
	1−				

2÷		30×	9+		2÷
3+	6		3÷		
	25×		2÷	5+	
		9+		2÷	11+
1−			5−		
2÷				4−	

Puzzle 1 (6×6):

2÷		120×		5+	
75×			4−		5−
2÷			5+		
		11+		3−	5+
48×		3÷			
		6	12+		

Puzzle 2 (6×6):

8+		2÷		30×	
11+		5−		36×	3−
	3+				
1−	1−		120×	3÷	3÷
	10×	3÷			
2				5+	

12×		3+		90×	
2−		5	5−		
3−	5+		5+		7+
	2÷		4−	48×	
6×	7+				
	6	1−		3−	

4−	4	2÷		8×	24×
	9+	11+			
3÷			3+		
		7+	2÷		6+
2÷			1−	90×	
2÷					

Puzzle 1 (135)

2−	15×		6+	2÷	
	5−				20×
30×		3÷	5−		
	3−		8+		5−
4−		24×	1−	3÷	
					3

Puzzle 2 (136)

72×		10×		5−	
	2÷	2	80×	4−	
3−		1−			
	3+		2÷		2−
20×		5−	30×	18×	

2÷		120×	2÷		6+
13+			9+	3	
		11+		18×	
3+				2−	
1−	5−		150×		2÷

1−		300×			6
5−	2−	2÷		90×	
			4	5+	
360×			5−		7+
7+		90×		8+	

Puzzle 139

5−	11+		12+		24×
	15×			3÷	
1−		16×	5−		
				5+	30×
6+		90×			
2	2−				

Puzzle 140

6+	20×	1−		5−	2÷
			40×		
5−				3	1−
11+	3÷		3÷		
		5−		1−	2÷
3÷		15×			

12+	11+		5−	6×	2÷
		12×			
20×			7+	7+	120×
3+	1−				
	5−		7+	1−	
9+					3

24×	2÷		15×	11+	
				2÷	
6		2−	5−	11+	
3+				1−	
90×		2÷			2÷
	11+		3−		

1
4
3

Puzzle 143

2÷		2−		5	6+
20×	2−	3−	3+	5−	
					9+
	11+	2−			
6+		5+	24×		4−
			2−		

1
4
4

Puzzle 144

10×	9+		5−		1−
		3÷	1−		
6	16+		5+	3−	2−
3÷					
	16×	3÷		4−	
		1−		1−	

Puzzle 145

45×	5	2÷	24×		
			2÷		3÷
15+			3−	30×	
5−	6+				
		14+			1−
7+			11+		

Puzzle 146

30×				11+	
2÷	1−		5−		3−
	288×			6×	
		10×	1−		
6+	2÷			90×	4
		10+			

77

Puzzle 147

13+		3÷		50×	
	1	3÷			2−
11+	1−		3÷		
	11+		3−		3
2÷		14+	5	5−	
				2−	

Puzzle 148

3+		2÷		24×	1−
100×	5−				
		3+		2÷	
6	2−		3−		4−
1−	2÷		1	15×	
	120×				

Puzzle 1:

2÷		15×		5−	
20×	3÷		15×		
	2÷		3−	1−	3÷
3+		4−			
2−			48×		
5−		2÷		2−	

149

Puzzle 2:

1−	6×		30×		72×
	3+		3÷		
5−	2−	240×		3÷	
					3−
5+	5		1−	3−	
	2÷				1

150

79

151

60×		3−	2÷	6+	
11+				3	3÷
	12×			1−	
	3−		8+		72×
10+	7+				
		6+		2÷	

152

10×		32×	14+		7+
				1−	
12+			48×		2−
3÷					
72×	3÷		12+	5−	2−

80

Puzzle 1 (6×6)

3−	11+	1	12×	3÷	
		10×		1−	1−
1−					
11+	11+			1−	
	1−	3−	3−		3−
2			4−		

Puzzle 2 (6×6)

108×		4−		2÷	
2−		19+	9+	3÷	
					40×
3−			1−		
8+	3+			10+	
	2÷		1−		

155

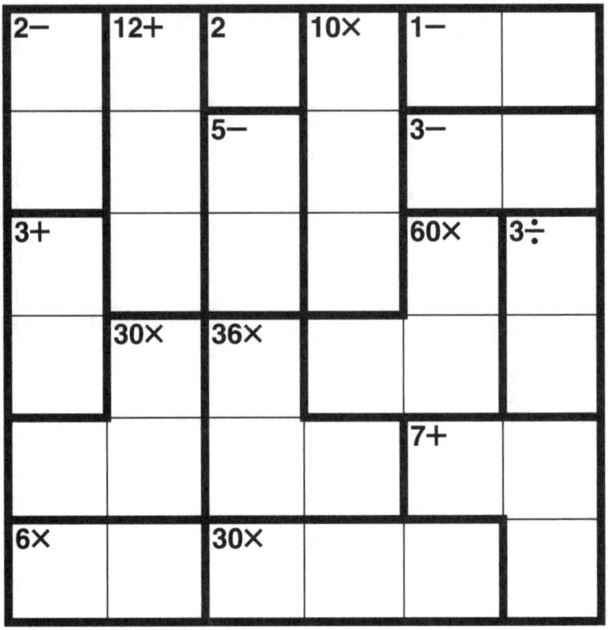
2−
12+
2
10×
1−
5−
3−
3+
60×
3÷
30×
36×
7+
6×
30×

156

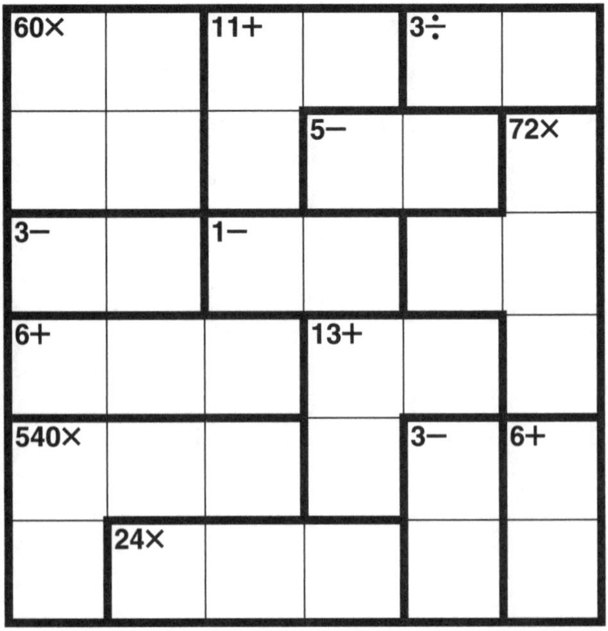
60×
11+
3÷
5−
72×
3−
1−
6+
13+
540×
3−
6+
24×

Puzzle 157

3−	12×	2÷		7+	
		2÷		11+	
2−	1	2÷		3−	
	150×		2÷		12×
3÷		9+	5−		
			1−		

Puzzle 158

11+	72×	3−		1−	
			13+	2÷	
3	1−				16+
96×			3÷		
	6+		3	1−	
3÷		3÷			

83

159

60×	12+		1	15×	
			3÷		2÷
11+			60×	2÷	
3+					20×
2÷	3−	2−		11+	
		2÷			

160

48×			13+	3	2÷
4	5−				
6+	2÷	2−	2−		1−
			3÷		
2−		24×	2÷	5−	
1−				1−	

Puzzle 161 (6×6):

2−		2÷	7+	90×	
120×					1−
3÷			5−	2	
	11+			2÷	
3−			5+		6
3÷		1−		4−	

Puzzle 162 (6×6):

11+	5+		6×	1−	
	1−	2−		4−	
			5−		3
5−		3−		96×	
2÷	4−		2−		
	2−			2÷	

163

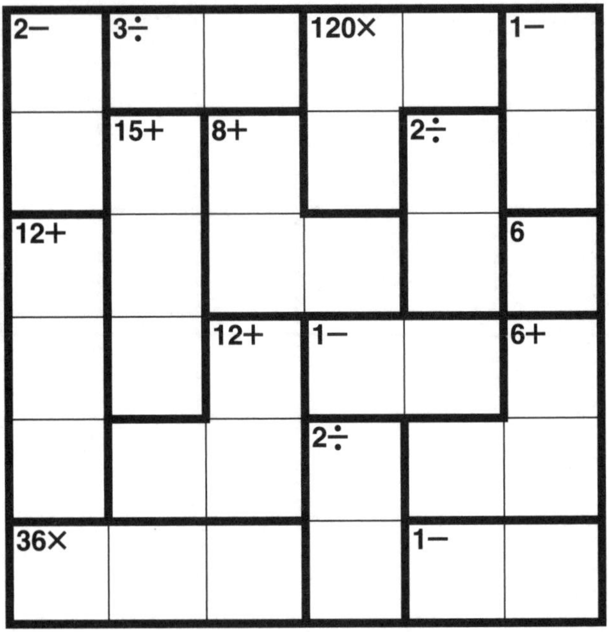
2−
3÷
120×
1−
15+
8+
2÷
12+
6
12+
1−
6+
2÷
36×
1−

164

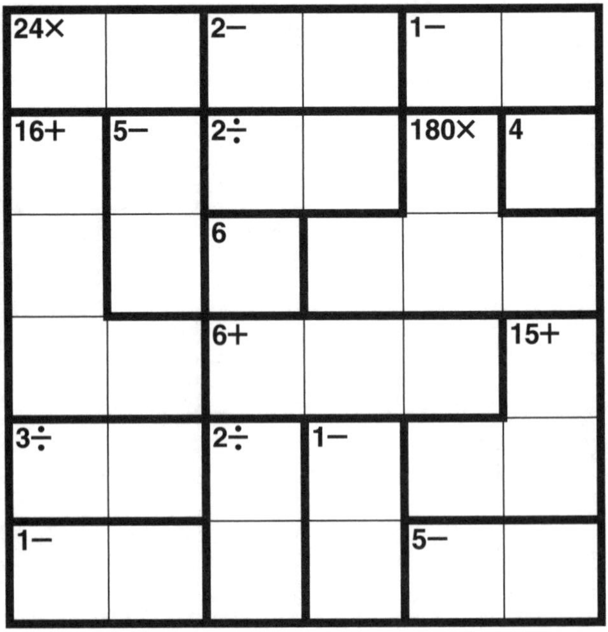
24×
2−
1−
16+
5−
2÷
180×
4
6
6+
15+
3÷
2÷
1−
1−
5−

4−		24×		12+	
2−		9+			3−
8+	3−	5			
		6+		5−	
3÷	6×	1−		20×	
			11+		

5+		90×		3÷	
6+	3−	480×		2−	
				3÷	30×
	2÷				
1−	13+		1−	2−	
					4

6×	1−		30×	3÷	
	30×			3÷	2÷
5+	7+				
		15+			30×
11+	6+		5−	1−	

3	1−	5−	11+		2÷
2÷			2−	15×	
	2÷				1−
15+	2−		2−		
	3÷	60×		4−	
				1−	

Puzzle 169

3+	2−	2÷		1−	
		2÷		3−	
48×		1−		1	3÷
		5	1−		
1−		1−		1−	
48×			4−		3

Puzzle 170

2−		5−		180×	
2÷	20×	1−			
		2÷		16+	
11+		6+			
2÷	4−		2÷		
	1−		8+		

171

5−		2÷	60×		
1−			24×	8+	
2−	2−				15+
	3−		7+		
2÷	24×		9+		
	36×				1

172

1−		3÷		6+	
2÷	5−		20×		6×
	2−			6	
6+	2÷	2−	11+		
			5	1−	
2÷		3−		3−	

Puzzle 173

3÷	30×	5+		1−	
			120×	3÷	
2÷				2−	12×
13+	2÷				
	3−	10×		5−	
		1−			2

Puzzle 174

3÷		2÷	120×	90×	
2÷					
10+		14+			
2−		11+		2÷	
	24×	2−		6+	2−
5					

6×		18+	1−	10+	1−
20×	5				
				10+	
3÷	1−		20×		
	15+			1−	
2−		3÷		3−	

3−	15+			6×	
	2÷		72×	30×	
5−		2÷			1−
2−					
60×		6×		5+	
	2−		2−		1

Puzzle 177

60×		2−		2	4−
8×		10+	5−		
	2−		48×		
			13+	120×	
1−	2÷				
	2−			3÷	

Puzzle 178

3÷		75×	8+		
3+			60×		10+
	12×	10+	6		
					2−
8+	14+		9+		
				4−	

Puzzle 179

4−	3÷		60×		6+
	1−			12+	
1	2−	20×			
90×				1−	
		8+		3÷	2−
9+					

Puzzle 180

36×	5−		12+		
		10×			3−
2−		3÷		1−	
3−		2−	2		6×
6+			2÷		
4	1−		30×		

Puzzle 1

60×	24×	4−		36×	2÷
	2÷	3−		6×	8+
3+		40×			
	2−			16+	
2÷		2÷			

Puzzle 2

720×					1
15+		36×		3÷	
			72×		200×
2÷	5−				
	216×		10×	12+	

Puzzle 183

40×	5−	2÷		2÷	
		3+		2−	
	60×	1−	5+		5−
			2−	1−	
2÷		5			6×
13+			5		

Puzzle 184

1−		72×			4−
10+		3÷		11+	
	1−				2÷
90×	6×		6+	1−	
		48×			4
			6+		

Puzzle 185

96×	15+		2−		7+
			3÷		
	9+		2÷		3−
		2÷	1−	4×	
	50×				
		10+			4

Puzzle 186

5−		1−		2÷	180×
2−	48×				
	10×			15+	
9+	7+		3÷		
		20×			3−
1−			1−		

30×	60×			1−	
	2÷		1−	10+	
2÷	4−	2÷		15+	
			5−		1−
12×	9+	4			
			5	5+	

30×			20×		5−
1−	15+	1−		18×	
					7+
18×		12+			
	2÷	7+		1−	
			1−		5

189

4×	15+			1−	
		2−		9+	2÷
7+	1−				
		1	15+		
108×		2÷		1−	
5		1−		3−	

190

1−		1−	3÷		8×
11+			9+		
13+		3+	288×	13+	
	4−				2−
2÷		2÷		1	

191

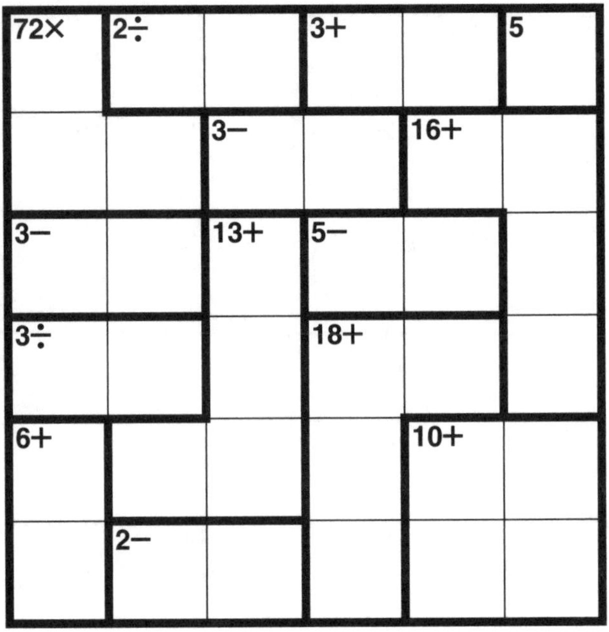

192

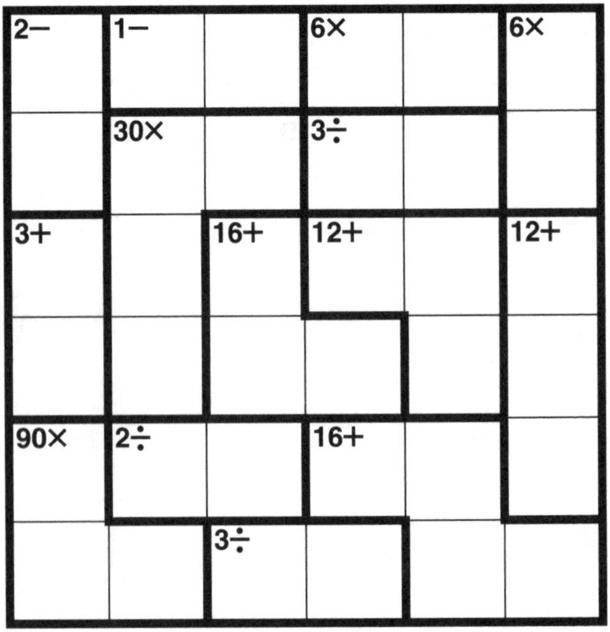

Puzzle 193

14+		3÷		40×	
12×		2÷		12+	
	5−		12+		
11+				108×	
1	2÷				
1−		30×			2

Puzzle 194

4×		11+		19+	
	2−				
15+				6×	4
2÷	16+	2÷			
			7+		9+
48×					

1−		3−		1−	
30×	2÷		1	2÷	
		2−		2÷	
9+	6+			1−	20×
	4	4−			
	8+		5−		

36×	5−		7+	1−	
		2÷		2	3−
4−	1−		2−	14+	
		24×			
1−				6×	
40×			5−		

Puzzle 197

8+		2−	6×		3
15+			10+	5−	
	2÷			10+	
		24×		20×	
2−	5+				
	13+			1−	

Puzzle 198

3÷		11+		8×	
4−	2÷		8+		
	1−		24×		36×
60×	30×				
		3+		1−	30×
	2	2−			

1 9 9

Puzzle 199 (6×6 grid)

2−	24×	1−		5−	
			2÷		11+
6×		11+	8+		
11+	2÷			3−	
		1−		3÷	1−
	13+				

2 0 0

Puzzle 200 (6×6 grid)

1−	12×			8+	
	7+		3÷	20×	
5−	2−				1−
	1−	4−	7+		
8+			36×	5−	
				4−	

3÷	1−	1−		3−	
		8+	3−	30×	
5−				3−	3÷
7+		11+	13+		
6+				1−	
1−				2−	

20×			2÷		2÷
24×	11+	2−	2÷		
			24×		
	3÷	3÷	11+		30×
			1−		
12+				6+	

2÷	1−	20×		2÷	
		10+		8+	2
2−			5−		10+
	3÷	16×			
5−				10+	4−
	2−				

12×			11+		3−
3÷		5+		48×	
2−	7+				2÷
	5−		1−		
5−	2−	2−		3−	5+
			6		

205

5−		2÷	20×		1−
1−			1−		
1−	3−	5+		11+	
		2÷		2÷	
2÷	1−	15+		3÷	6+
		3			

206

3÷		1−	20×		
13+			12+	5−	
	3+			15+	1−
15×		11+			
	20×		1−	2÷	
				3−	

2÷	7+	20×		7+	9+
		2÷			
5−		1−	1−		
3−			7+		11+
9+			10+		
2	1−			6+	

36×		4	3÷		13+
4−		3−			
	1−		13+		
3÷		11+		2÷	3−
2−	120×		15×		
				3÷	

209

1−	6+			30×	
	3÷	14+			4
6×			1−	3−	2÷
	4×				
		1−		1−	
1−		3	7+		

210

4−	6+			2÷	1−
	24×	3÷			
1−		1−		1	36×
		4−	1−		
3÷			1−		
2	15×		24×		

2÷	15×		3÷	2÷	
		1−		4−	
3−	3÷		10+		9+
		3÷	2−		
3−	3−			2	13+
		4−			

1−		2÷		30×	
5+	15+			6×	
	11+		12+	2÷	
3÷	2÷	2−			20×
			24×		
15×		2−			1

213

2÷	20×	11+	5−		7+
				12+	
3	9+		5+		12×
360×					
		3−	90×		
5−				7+	

214

6×		24×	2−		4
			1−		48×
14+	6+				
		2÷	2÷	7+	
9+				2÷	2−
	120×				

Puzzle 215 (6×6):

15+	2÷		12×		15×
	2÷	20×		12×	
					12+
2−		2÷			
13+		1−	2−		
			30×		

Puzzle 216 (6×6):

2−	2÷		450×		
	3	13+			
19+				12+	
180×			6×		
	60×				6+
		11+			

112

Puzzle 1 (217)

20×	360×			5−	
			12×		1
1−	8+			2−	
		1−	2÷	1−	
36×				1−	3−
	6+				

Puzzle 2 (218)

5−	54×		15+		
	15+			13+	
		8×			
	4		1−	12+	
12×	11+				2÷
			3÷		

219

15+	20×		3−		3÷
	5−		8+		
		3÷		3−	11+
30×			11+		
		1−		180×	
5+					

220

120×				1−	
3	7+		30×		
1−		1−		8+	15+
	6×	2−			
			7+		
3÷		1−		3÷	

1−	48×	5−		8+	
		2−	4−	60×	
15×				48×	
		2÷			6+
3÷	4−				
		2−		2−	

2
2
1

5+		3−	2−		2÷
3÷	4−		6	1−	
		10×	3−		3÷
2÷				15+	
1−					
14+				5−	

2
2
2

115

2−		3÷	3÷	2−	
11+				20×	2
	8+		11+		
2	5+			2÷	
5−		5		1−	
9+			12+		

5−		20×		2−	2÷
1−	1−		3÷		
	2−			5−	
2÷	2÷		3−	8+	
	6+			3÷	
2	7+		12+		

Puzzle 225

3−	2÷		1−	3−	1−
	24×	3÷			
			3÷		11+
8+	2	2−			
	2−	3−		2−	
		2−		3÷	

Puzzle 226

3÷	20×		2÷		3÷
		36×	14+		
8+	4−				
		4−		2−	
	15×	2÷		30×	
		72×			2

6+		6	1−		3−
1−		6×		2÷	
9+	4−		2−		3÷
	24×	15×		30×	
3÷					2−
			8+		

72×			120×		24×
1−	4−				
	3	21+			
7+	2÷				
	15+			9+	
		48×			

Puzzle 229

3−	24×	1	1−		5−
		18+	1−		
			5	1−	
12×	1−		3÷	1−	
	2−			12+	1−
	3÷				

Puzzle 230

1−		120×			17+
5−		9×			
9+					3÷
16+		1−			
	13+		3÷		24×
			5		

Puzzle 231

2÷	5−		2÷		30×
	1−		8+		
10+		3		16+	
3−	1−	3−			
			2÷		5−
8+			1−		

Puzzle 232

30×			2÷	3÷	5+
13+		15+			
9+				14+	1
	6+				
	12+			12+	
1−		30×			

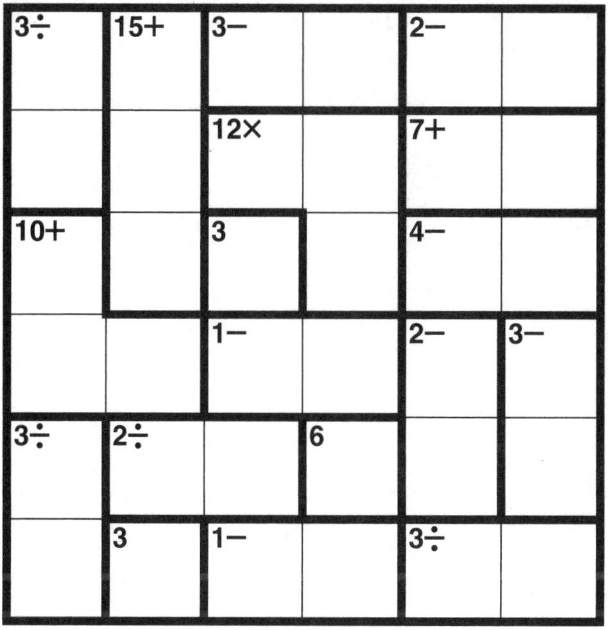
3÷
15+
3−
2−
12×
7+
10+
3
4−
1−
2−
3−
3÷
2÷
6
3
1−
3÷

2
3
3

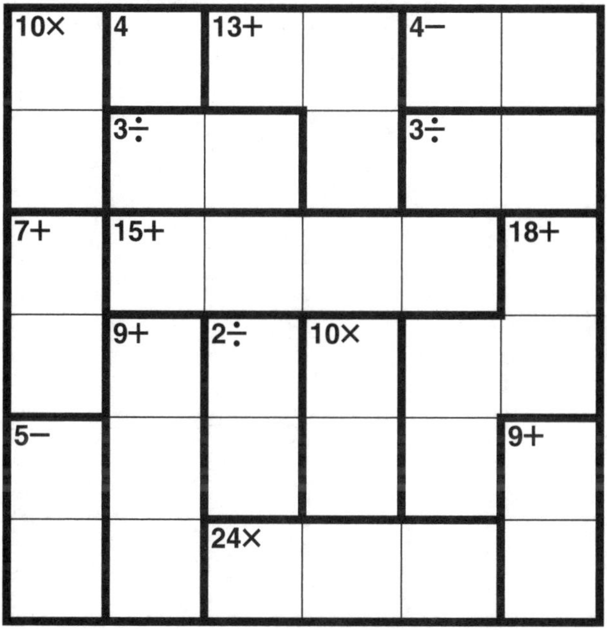
10×
4
13+
4−
3÷
3÷
7+
15+
18+
9+
2÷
10×
5−
9+
24×

2
3
4

2
3
5

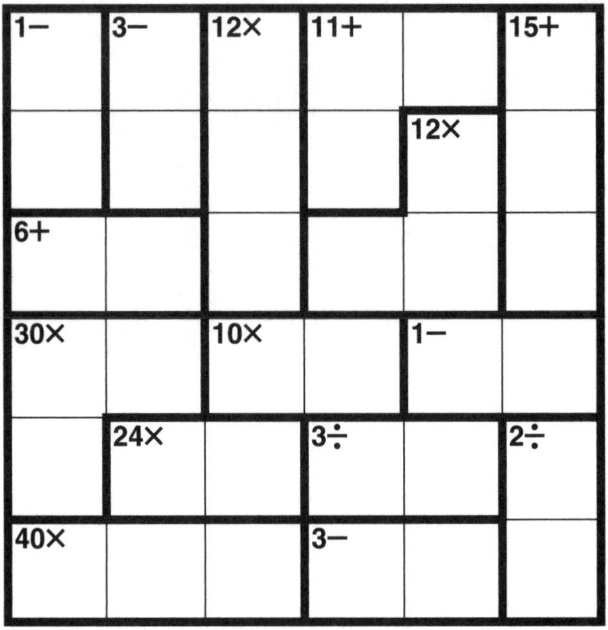

2
3
6

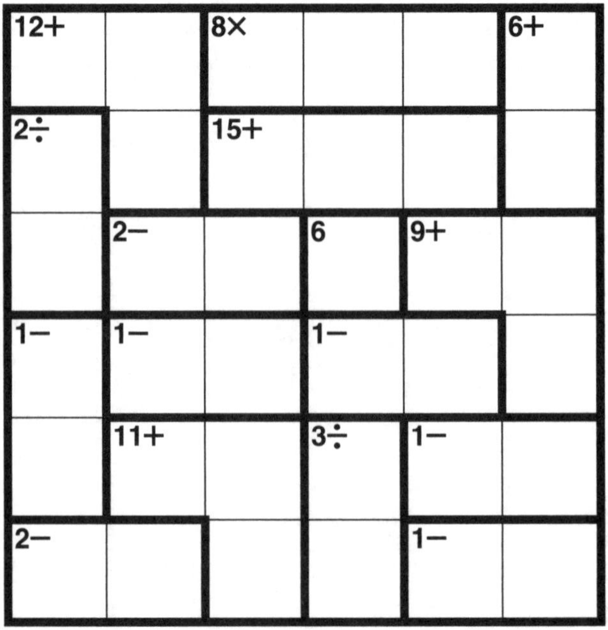

Puzzle 237

2−	2÷		1−	10×	
	9+				
9+	12×		1−		15+
			2÷		
	11+	10×			
		5−		1−	

Puzzle 238

32×		3÷	8+		4−
2−			5−		
	7+		80×		1−
2÷		20×			
2÷	6+	7+			3÷
			3−		

8×	15+	1−	18×		
			13+		8+
		30×			
12+			1−		11+
		3−		2	
5	2÷		2÷		

1	30×			2−	
2−	1−		4−		10+
	5−	2÷			
2−		4	7+	7+	
	5+			1−	5−
3−		2−			

Puzzle 1

2÷	30×	7+			1−
			2÷	15+	
3−	2÷				2÷
	1−		1−		
1−		13+		1−	1−
4					

2
4
1

Puzzle 2

2−	5−		3−		15+
	60×	12×			
			5+		12×
17+		1−		1−	
		2÷	1−		
1−				3÷	

2
4
2

Puzzle 243

5	4−		12×		
3−	9+	15+		3−	
		3÷		15+	
3÷			13+		
6+		4			
	8+		24×		1

Puzzle 244

1	72×			12+	
1−	15+		18×		2÷
				10+	
3÷		6			9+
	10+		1−		
1−				2−	

Grid 1 (cage clues):

10×		11+	2÷	3÷	
120×				6×	
4+			1−		15+
		12+		2÷	
13+					
	2−		8+		

Side label: 2 / 4 / 5

Grid 2 (cage clues):

36×	8+			180×	
	5−				20×
	12+	3÷	15+		
				2÷	
10×		8+		2÷	
4				3÷	

Side label: 2 / 4 / 6

247

2	40×			3−	
20×		5−	2−		8+
	13+		6×		
			10×		
2÷	12×			80×	
	30×				

248

48×	5−		1−	30×	
	12+			5−	
		60×	1		3÷
30×			1−		
	6+		16+	2	2−

Puzzle 1

40×	11+			3−	
		1−	15×	3÷	
4−					2−
15×			24×		
7+	5−			1−	3−
		2÷			

Puzzle 2

2÷		1−	60×		5+
11+					
	6	2×		1−	
15×			2÷		360×
4−		1−	36×		
3−					

5+	3−	24×		14+	
		2÷			6+
72×			12+	2÷	
30×					4
	5−	9+		15+	
		2÷			

20×	5+	15×		4−	24×
		1−			
	2÷	1−		4−	1−
2÷		1−			
	3÷		11+		9+
3−		4			

Puzzle 253

5−		60×			15+
2÷		11+	1−	3−	
24×					
	20×	2	3÷		
		11+	120×		
15×					1

Puzzle 254

2÷		15+			12×
1−		2÷	30×		
1−	2÷				6×
		3−	12×		
9+				9+	5
6		5+			

2−	3÷		15+	3÷	
	3÷			2÷	3−
3÷	40×				
		6	6+	1−	
3−	2−			2−	2÷
		3−			

5−		14+	1−		1−
3÷			1−	5	
	24×			6+	
40×		2−		3÷	
	2−	20×		5−	
		1	11+		

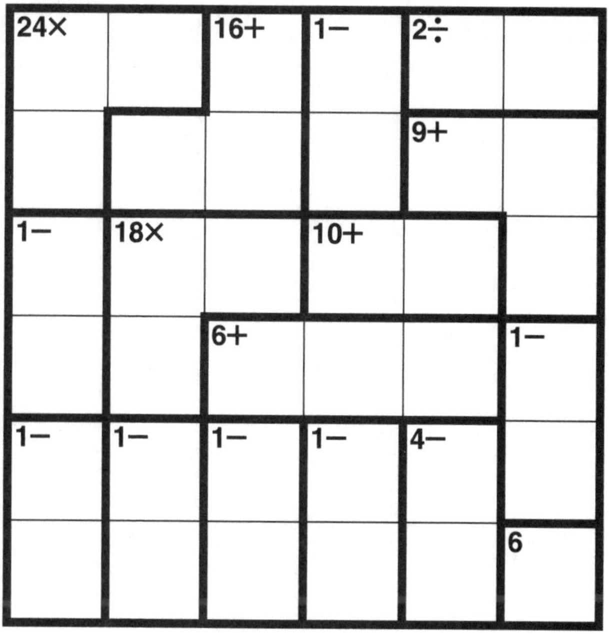
24×
16+
1−
2÷
9+
1−
18×
10+
6+
1−
1−
1−
1−
1−
4−
6

2
5
7

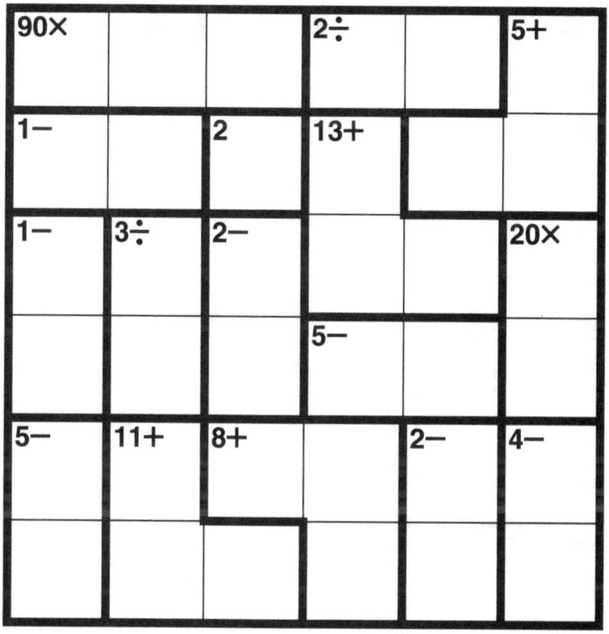
90×
2÷
5+
1−
2
13+
1−
3÷
2−
20×
5−
5−
11+
8+
2−
4−

2
5
8

1−	6+			48×	
	1−	2−		2÷	
1−		2−			3÷
	12+			1−	
7+	2	5+			11+
	2−		2−		

3÷		10×		11+	
3−				5	
3−		3−		10×	
15×	3−		2−		
		1−	2÷		14+
2−					

2÷		40×		2÷	
17+		18×		3÷	
				1−	90×
2−	7+				
	11+	6+	3−	3÷	
					4

2	2÷		20×		
4−		1−	2÷		2−
11+			2−		
2−		3÷		60×	1−
6×	1−				
		1−		5−	

Top puzzle (6×6)

3−	2−	150×		12+	
					2−
3÷	60×		1−		
		24×		2−	
1−			15+		5×
5+					

Bottom puzzle (6×6)

2−		2÷		24×	
2÷		14+			4
2−		6×	60×	3−	
2−	7+			9+	
		13+			3÷
6			1−		

Puzzle 265

4−		5+		2−	
4−		1−		2−	
6×	1−	5	5+		40×
		2−		3÷	
15+	2÷		1−		
				1	

Puzzle 266

2÷		2÷		5−	6+
1−		18+			
120×					12+
	4−	11+			
7+		9+		10+	
		5			

Puzzle 2 6 7

2÷		5−		15×	
7+		1−		10+	
2−		2−	13+		2÷
15×	3				
	7+	7+		13+	5−

Puzzle 2 6 8

40×	1−		1−		4
		2÷		4−	
	5−		30×	2÷	
14+				2−	
		11+		6×	1−
2	1−				

6×	2−		1−		13+
	1−		2÷		
5	4−			6×	
3−		3−			5+
5−	2÷	3−	3−	13+	

3−		2÷	30×	2÷	
12×				11+	6+
	1−	11+	2−		
2−					
	3−		8×	5−	1−
1−					

Puzzle 271

120×		56×			90×	
		15×		6−	13+	
48×						
6×	15×			17+	2÷	17+
	6−					
1−	30×		56×	2−		
				4	4−	

Puzzle 272

5+		1−	4−	30×	2÷	5+
84×						
3÷		11+		3−	13+	6+
	6×		2−			
3÷	6−			1−	9+	17+
	14+	4−	2÷			
				2−		

Puzzle 2 7 3

13+	6−		1−		6×	
	13+		24×		3÷	
7+			5−	3÷	5	14+
3÷	3÷				120×	
	3−		5−			
3−	60×			8+		2−
		3÷		14×		

Puzzle 2 7 4

1−	13+		1−		2÷	
	144×	5	6−		18×	3−
5−						
	6−		4−	1−		2÷
11+		14+		4−	18+	
5−						
	2÷		3	16+		

3÷	140×	6−		12+	10×	
			19+			
21×						24×
3+		2−		13+		
60×	168×	7+		8+		
			2÷	2	18+	
	3−			5+		

1−	1470×		3−		10+	10+
	2÷		20×	14×		
3−						
	1−		13+		9+	21×
14+		3÷	2÷	140×		
	18+					4−
		12×		3+		

Puzzle 1

10+	4−		24×	378×		
	25+			1	8+	
3÷				11+		
	2÷	2÷			35×	
35×		2÷		6−		10+
	2−		10+			
2	11+			10+		

2 7 7

Puzzle 2

30×	13+		3+		96×	
			11+	1−	13+	
6+						2−
6−	2÷	3−		2÷		
		6×		10+		
24×		60×		35×	5+	
2÷		7				

2 7 8

Puzzle 279

32×		105×	15+			
	14+			3+		7
13+		4−	10+	10+		3+
				2−		
42×		2÷		3−	4−	9+
		1−				
6+		1−		4	1−	

Puzzle 280

3÷		1−		2−	35×	
2	6−	5−			60×	
11+		5−	11+	12+		
				13+	3+	24×
	40×					
23+		5+	18+	1−		1−

Puzzle 1 (6×6):

1−		168×		10+		1−
8+	2÷		16+	12×		
					5+	
10×	2−	6+	2−		12+	
			15+			
4−			28×	6×		1−
7+				10×		

Puzzle 2 (6×6):

4−	140×		2−		5−	1−
		126×	2÷			
6	6+		3−		15+	
84×			3÷	2−		
				5−		
	17+	6+			12×	1−
			4−			

283

14+		11+	60×		15+	
			504×			
6+	1−					14×
	2−		6−	1−		
	8+				1−	2÷
5	20+		18×			
		2÷			1−	

284

12×			22+	16+		
1−				6−		
	4−		504×		84×	
24×		6−				8+
210×			20×			
	3−		10+	14+		
	3÷					

146

Puzzle 285

21×		3+	11+	13+	1−	3−
4						
3÷	14+	30×			42×	
			4−			2−
9+			22+	10+		
1−					6+	
6+		7+				7

Puzzle 286

24×		3+		2−	10×	1−
7	1−	120×				
21×			3÷	2÷		12+
		11+			17+	
1−	2					3−
	6−		3−			
3−		1−		1	1−	

2 8 7

14+		1−		2÷		16+
	5	42×		2−		
	13+	12×	10×		1−	
				5+		4
	120×	12+			15×	5−
				42×		
28×		3÷			7+	

2 8 8

1−	4−		3−		3−	
	2÷	1−	13+	24×		2×
6−						
	60×	12+		1−	90×	
					2−	
2−	2÷	5−	13+	3		11+
					7	

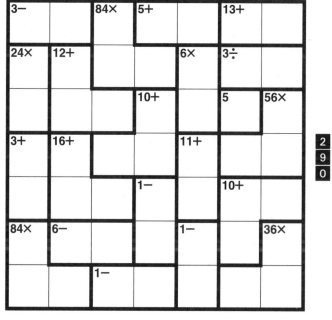

Puzzle 291

210×			105×	7+		
2÷	10+				10+	
	2−			60×		
6+	280×		4−	10+		3−
				126×		
2÷	2÷	1−			3−	21×
		3−				

Puzzle 292

60×			3−	6−	60×	
12+					2÷	
12+		3−		4−		56×
2÷		15×				
	1−	5−		2−	4−	
20+		3÷			3−	
		1−		4	6+	

Puzzle 293

24×		84×		1	11+	
5−		1−		20+		
	2−		56×			
17+		18+			16×	
		4−		24×		
	35×		3−			6×
2−				2÷		

Puzzle 294

8+		1−		50×	10+	
7+	3÷				3−	
		19+		3÷	2−	5−
1−	7+					
	4−	2÷	140×			5+
13+			11+	3−		
					3−	

2÷		5−		6+	105×	
17+		140×				
	3−				11+	
1−	3	14+		5+		
	2−			13+	10+	
3−		3÷			7+	
3	9+			140×		

4−		12×	5−	15+		
15×	14×				6+	
		35×		24×		1−
1−		3÷			3÷	
18+		5−				16+
	6+		2−	2−		
		5			1−	

Puzzle 297:

4−		2÷		105×	13+	
2÷		10+			3−	
105×				2÷	8+	
		2−			56×	
504×	1−	2−	6−			
			6×	5−		15×
				1−		

Puzzle 298:

84×			17+	5+		1−
2÷	36×					
	7+		14+	210×		1
6+		210×			2−	
					5−	
8+		8×	1−		168×	1−
15×						

297

298

153

12×			2−		2÷	16+
12+		3−	3÷	4		
13+				35×		
	4	3−	14+			
	6−			6×		
6+		6×		168×		4−
	1−		2÷			

36×	3−		1−		2÷	
	5	3−		6+	3−	8+
	10+					
1−		9+	84×		5	
6+					4−	1−
8+	1−		12+			
	5−			12+		

1

2− 1	3	1− 4	4− 5	1− 2
3− 2	2÷ 4	5	1	3
5	2	12× 3	4	1
2− 3	5	6+ 1	2	1− 4
3− 4	1	2 2	3	5

2

15× 5	3	5+ 2	3− 4	1
2÷ 1	2	3	2− 5	9+ 4
2− 2	1 1	10+ 4	3	5
4	5	1	6× 2	3
1− 3	4	8+ 5	1	2

3

4+ 1	4− 5	3 3	2÷ 2	4
3	1	1− 4	5	3− 2
120× 4	3	1− 2	1	5
5	2	4− 1	1− 4	2− 3
2÷ 2	4	5	3	1

4

6+ 2	6+ 5	2− 3	1	2÷ 4
3	1	1− 4	5	2
1	2÷ 4	2	9+ 3	15× 5
20× 5	2÷ 2	1	4	3
4	2− 3	5	2	1

5

5+ 1	4	1− 2	9+ 5	2− 3
2÷ 2	1	3	4	5
60× 3	3− 2	5	3− 1	4
4	4− 5	1	1− 3	2
5	1− 3	4	2÷ 2	1

6

2÷ 2	60× 5	3	4	1
1	3 3	16+ 5	2	4
3− 4	1	2÷ 2	5	10+ 3
9+ 5	4	1	8+ 3	2
1− 3	2	4	1	5

7

2÷ 2	1	24× 4	3	5 5
4 4	12+ 5	2	6+ 1	3
6+ 1	4	2− 3	5	2
5	3	8× 1	2	4
30× 3	2	5	3− 4	1

8

40× 2	5	4	5+ 1	3
1− 4	3+ 2	2− 5	3	1
5	1	1− 3	2	11+ 4
12× 3	4	4− 1	5	2
2− 1	3	2÷ 2	4	5

155

9

11+ 2	4	6× 3	4− 5	1
5	2÷ 1	2	10+ 3	4
2− 1	2	9+ 5	5+ 4	3
3	13+ 5	4	1	9+ 2
4	3	1	2	5

10

9+ 4	1− 3	10× 2	5	1
5	2	3− 4	1	30× 3
2− 3	5+ 4	1	2 2	5
1	5 5	12+ 3	4	2
2÷ 2	1	5	1− 3	4

11

1− 3	2÷ 1	2	1− 5	4
2	1− 4	5	1− 3	10× 1
6+ 1	2	3	4	5
2− 5	3	6+ 4	1	2
1− 4	5	1	6× 2	3

12

6+ 3	40× 4	2	6+ 5	1
1	3	2− 5	2÷ 2	4
2	1	8+ 4	15× 3	5
1− 4	8+ 5	3	1	1− 2
5	2	1	4 4	3

13

2÷ 2	1	2− 3	5	60× 4
8+ 1	10+ 4	5 5	1− 2	3
3	2	4	1	5
4	15× 5	1	6+ 3	2
5 5	3	2− 2	4	1

14

10+ 5	1	1− 4	3	24× 2
4	2÷ 2	1	4− 5	3
1− 2	2− 5	3	1	4
3	20× 4	5	2÷ 2	1
6× 1	3	2	1− 4	5

15

2− 4	2	5 5	4− 1	1− 3
6+ 3	2÷ 1	2	5	4
2	1− 5	1− 4	3	1 1
1	4	2− 3	10× 2	5
2− 5	3	1	2− 4	2

16

60× 3	1	4	2÷ 2	5 5
5	8+ 2	2− 3	1	5+ 4
2	4	5	7+ 3	1
3− 1	2− 5	1− 2	4	1− 3
4	3	1	5 5	2

156

17

2÷ **2**	11+ **3**	20× **5**	**4**	**1**
1	**5**	**3**	8+ **2**	1− **4**
14+ **5**	**2**	5+ **4**	**1**	**3**
3	8× **4**	**1**	**5**	2 **2**
4	**1**	**2**	2− **3**	**5**

18

2− **3**	2÷ **1**	2− **5**	2− **4**	**2**
1	**2**	**3**	4− **5**	1− **4**
24× **2**	**3**	10+ **4**	**1**	**5**
4	**5**	**1**	1− **2**	4+ **3**
1− **5**	**4**	2 **2**	**3**	**1**

19

4+ **3**	2÷ **2**	1− **4**	**5**	2÷ **1**
1	**4**	60× **5**	**3**	**2**
2− **5**	**3**	8× **2**	**1**	**4**
40× **2**	**5**	**1**	**4**	2− **3**
4	6+ **1**	**3**	**2**	**5**

20

7+ **1**	1− **4**	2 **2**	15× **5**	**3**
2	**5**	4+ **3**	1− **4**	**1**
4	2÷ **2**	**1**	**3**	40× **5**
2− **3**	**1**	8+ **5**	**2**	**4**
5	**3**	1− **4**	**1**	**2**

21

12+ **4**	**2**	**5**	36× **1**	**3**
2÷ **2**	30× **5**	**1**	**3**	**4**
1	**3**	**2**	1− **4**	**5**
2− **5**	1− **4**	**3**	2 **2**	10× **1**
3	3− **1**	**4**	**5**	**2**

22

20× **4**	8+ **2**	**5**	2− **3**	**1**
5	**1**	9+ **2**	**4**	**3**
6+ **1**	**5**	1− **3**	**2**	2÷ **4**
24× **3**	**4**	7+ **1**	**5**	**2**
2	**3**	1− **4**	**1**	5 **5**

23

8× **4**	**2**	**1**	2− **3**	**5**
8+ **3**	2− **1**	3− **5**	**2**	4 **4**
5	**3**	2÷ **2**	**4**	6+ **1**
2÷ **2**	1− **5**	3− **4**	**1**	**3**
1	**4**	2− **3**	**5**	**2**

24

10× **2**	**5**	2÷ **4**	8+ **1**	**3**
1	1− **3**	**2**	3− **5**	**4**
1− **5**	**4**	45× **3**	**2**	1− **1**
4	**1**	**5**	**3**	**2**
1− **3**	**2**	10+ **1**	**4**	**5**

2 5

2÷ 4	2	4+ 1	2− 3	5
2− 1	20× 5	3	2− 4	2
3	4	20× 5	8+ 2	1
2÷ 2	1	4	5	1− 3
2− 5	3	1− 2	1	4

2 6

1− 3	48× 1	5	2÷ 2	4
2	4	3	4− 1	5
2÷ 1	2	4	11+ 5	3
12+ 4	6+ 5	1	3	1− 2
5	3	2÷ 2	4	1

2 7

2− 3	5	2÷ 1	2	1− 4
2÷ 4	6× 1	2	3	5
2	1− 3	10+ 4	5	1
6+ 5	4	30× 3	2÷ 1	2
1	2	5	1− 4	3

2 8

2÷ 4	2	12× 3	4− 1	3− 5
10+ 3	4	1	5	2
2	5	40× 4	8+ 3	1
2− 1	3	5	2	4
10× 5	1	2	1− 4	3

2 9

1− 4	3	20× 5	1	8+ 2
5+ 3	2	4	5	1
2÷ 2	15× 5	1	3 3	40× 4
1	4 4	3	2	5
5 5	1− 1	2	1− 4	3

3 0

40× 5	2− 1	3	2÷ 2	4
4	2	4− 1	5	2− 3
1− 2	8+ 3	20× 5	4	1
1	5	4	1− 3	3− 2
1− 3	4	1− 2	1	5

3 1

6+ 1	2	3	1− 4	5
3− 5	12× 3	1− 4	2÷ 2	1
2	4	5	2− 1	3
12× 3	1	10× 2	2− 5	2÷ 4
4	5	1	3	2

3 2

1− 5	4	120× 3	2÷ 1	2
5+ 4	1	2	15× 5	3
2 2	5	4	1− 3	1
6+ 3	2	1	4	1− 5
2− 1	3	3− 5	2	4

33

³⁻1	¹⁰ˣ2	¹⁻5	4	¹⁻3
4	5	¹⁰⁺3	1	2
²⁻5	3	4	2	⁴⁻1
¹⁻2	³⁻4	²÷1	⁶⁰ˣ3	5
3	1	2	5	4

34

²⁰ˣ2	5	1	⁸⁺4	3
³⁻4	2	¹⁰ˣ5	²⁻3	1
1	²⁻3	2	5	⁴⁰ˣ4
²⁻3	1	²÷4	2	5
5	¹⁻4	3	1	2

35

⁶⁺1	¹²⁰ˣ4	3	2	5
2	3	¹¹⁺5	³⁻1	4
⁴4	5	1	²⁻3	²÷2
²⁻3	²÷2	²÷4	5	1
5	1	2	¹⁻4	3

36

¹⁻4	3	⁵5	²÷2	1
⁶⁺1	²÷2	4	³⁰ˣ3	5
3	⁶⁺5	1	¹³⁺4	2
2	1	3	5	⁷⁺4
¹⁻5	4	¹⁻2	1	3

37

²÷1	⁷⁵ˣ5	²÷2	4	¹²⁺3
2	3	5	²÷1	4
⁹⁺3	⁵⁺1	4	2	5
4	2	²⁻3	⁸⁺5	²÷1
5	4	1	3	2

38

³⁻2	5	¹⁵ˣ3	⁸⁺1	³⁻4
¹⁻4	3	5	2	1
²⁻3	⁷⁺1	4	5	²2
5	2	²÷1	¹⁻4	3
³⁻1	4	2	⁸⁺3	5

39

²⁰ˣ4	⁴⁻1	5	²⁻3	¹⁻2
5	²⁻4	2	1	3
1	²2	¹²⁺3	4	5
¹⁰⁺2	⁸⁺3	4	⁴⁻5	1
3	5	1	²÷2	4

40

¹³⁺5	²⁴ˣ2	3	4	²÷1
3	¹⁻5	4	²÷1	2
1	4	¹¹⁺5	2	⁶⁰ˣ3
²⁻2	3	1	5	4
4	¹1	2	²⁻3	5

159

4-1

2− 3	5	**75×** 1	**8+** 4	2
10+ 1	**1−** 3	5	2	**4** 4
4	2	3	5	**10+** 1
5	**2−** 4	2	1	3
2÷ 2	1	**1−** 4	3	5

4-2

3− 2	**60×** 3	**4−** 1	5	**4** 4
5	4	**9+** 2	1	**2−** 3
1− 3	5	4	2	1
4	**9+** 1	5	**1−** 3	2
2÷ 1	2	3	**1−** 4	5

4-3

30× 5	**40×** 4	2	**1** 1	**10+** 3
3	5	4	2	1
1	**1−** 2	3	**1−** 4	5
2	**2−** 3	1	**13+** 5	**2÷** 4
5+ 4	1	5	3	2

4-4

1− 2	3	**12×** 1	4	**10×** 5
9+ 4	5	3	2	1
1− 3	4	**9+** 5	1	**2÷** 2
8+ 5	**1** 1	**2÷** 2	3	4
1	2	4	**2−** 5	3

4-5

3− 4	1	**12+** 3	2	5
4− 1	**2÷** 4	**5** 5	**12×** 3	2
5	2	1	4	**8+** 3
1− 2	**2−** 3	**9+** 4	5	1
3	5	**2÷** 2	1	4

4-6

1− 4	3	**2÷** 2	1	**15×** 5
1− 5	4	**1−** 3	2	1
1 1	**2−** 2	4	**12+** 5	3
3− 2	5	**4−** 1	3	4
2− 3	1	5	**2÷** 4	2

4-7

20× 1	**2−** 5	3	**2÷** 4	2
4	**7+** 1	2	**15×** 3	5
5	4	**1−** 1	2	**12×** 3
1− 3	**3−** 2	5	**4−** 1	4
2	3	**1−** 4	5	1

4-8

2÷ 4	2	**3** 3	**4−** 1	5
10× 2	**1−** 3	4	**9+** 5	**2÷** 1
5	**10+** 4	1	3	2
4+ 3	1	5	**2÷** 2	4
1	**11+** 5	2	4	**3** 3

49

30×			5+	
5	**3**	**2**	**4**	**1**
1−	6+	2−		60×
4	**1**	**3**	**5**	**2**
3	**4**	**1**	**2**	**5**
2÷	10×			12×
1	**2**	**5**	**3**	**4**
2	1− **5**	**4**	**1**	**3**

50

10×	30×		11+	
1	**5**	**2**	**3**	**4**
5	1 **1**	**3**	**4**	2÷ **2**
2	24× **3**	20× **4**	**5**	**1**
1− **3**	**4**	**1**	8+ **2**	2− **5**
4	**2**	**5**	**1**	**3**

51

2−	3−		3−	
3	**5**	**2**	**1**	**4**
1	1− **4**	**5**	40× **2**	4+ **3**
3− **2**	3 **3**	**4**	**5**	**1**
5	2− **1**	**3**	2÷ **4**	**2**
2− **4**	**2**	9+ **1**	**3**	**5**

52

2−		40×		
1	**3**	**4**	**2**	**5**
2 **2**	9+ **5**	**3**	**1**	5+ **4**
12+ **3**	2÷ **2**	20× **5**	**4**	**1**
5	**4**	**1**	2− **3**	5+ **2**
4	2÷ **1**	**2**	**5**	**3**

53

4−	2−	1−		8×
1	**5**	**3**	**2**	**4**
5	**3**	5+ **4**	**1**	**2**
2÷ **2**	**4**	11+ **5**	**3**	**1**
4 **4**	**2**	**1**	11+ **5**	8+ **3**
2− **3**	**1**	**2**	**4**	**5**

54

2÷		2−		8×
1	**2**	**3**	**5**	**4**
1− **4**	**5**	4+ **1**	**3**	**2**
30× **5**	**3**	**2**	4 **4**	**1**
1− **3**	3− **1**	**4**	7+ **2**	**5**
2	**4**	1− **5**	**1**	2− **3**

55

30×	8+		1−	
2	**3**	**1**	**5**	**4**
5	**4**	2÷ **2**	**1**	6+ **3**
3	4− **5**	1− **4**	9+ **2**	**1**
3− **4**	**1**	**5**	**3**	**2**
1	1− **2**	**3**	**4**	5 **5**

56

24×		12+	1−	
1	**2**	**5**	**3**	**4**
4	**3**	**2**	**5**	2− **1**
1− **2**	20× **5**	**4**	**1**	**3**
3	20× **4**	2− **1**	3− **2**	**5**
5	**1**	**3**	2÷ **4**	**2**

57

3 ²⁻	**5**	**2** ⁴⁰ˣ	**4**	**1** ⁸ˣ
4 ⁵⁺	**1**	**5**	**3** ²⁻	**2**
2 ¹⁻	**3** ⁹⁺	**1** ¹	**5**	**4**
1	**4**	**3** ¹⁻	**2** ²÷	**5** ²⁻
5 ⁵	**2**	**4**	**1**	**3**

58

2 ²÷	**1**	**5** ¹³⁺	**3** ¹²ˣ	**4**
3 ¹⁻	**4**	**1**	**2**	**5**
4 ¹⁰⁺	**5** ⁸⁺	**3**	**1** ⁵⁺	**2** ⁶ˣ
5	**3** ¹⁻	**2**	**4**	**1**
1	**2** ²⁻	**4**	**5** ⁵	**3**

59

5 ¹⁵ˣ	**3** ⁸⁺	**2** ⁷⁺	**4**	**1**
1	**2**	**3**	**5** ¹⁻	**4**
3	**1** ¹⁰⁺	**4**	**2** ¹⁰ˣ	**5**
2 ²÷	**4**	**5**	**1**	**3** ¹⁻
4 ⁹⁺	**5**	**1** ⁴⁺	**3**	**2**

60

1 ³⁻	**2** ⁴⁰ˣ	**4**	**5**	**3** ⁹⁺
4	**3** ¹⁵ˣ	**2** ¹⁻	**1**	**5**
5	**1**	**3**	**4** ²÷	**2**
3 ¹⁻	**5** ¹⁻	**1** ¹⁻	**2**	**4** ⁵⁺
2	**4**	**5**	**3** ¹⁵ˣ	**1**

61

3 ⁶ˣ	**1** ⁶⁺	**5**	**2** ²÷	**4**
2	**4** ⁷⁺	**3**	**1** ¹⁰⁺	**5** ²⁻
1	**2** ²	**4** ⁵⁺	**5**	**3**
5 ¹⁻	**3** ²⁻	**1**	**4**	**2** ¹⁻
4	**5**	**2** ¹⁻	**3**	**1**

62

5 ¹⁰ˣ	**2** ²÷	**4**	**3** ²⁻	**1**
1	**3** ⁵⁺	**2**	**5** ¹⁻	**4** ¹⁻
2	**5** ⁴⁻	**1**	**4**	**3**
3 ¹⁻	**4**	**5** ⁹⁺	**1**	**2** ⁹⁺
4 ³⁻	**1**	**3**	**2**	**5**

63

3 ¹⁻	**4**	**1** ²÷	**2**	**5** ¹⁵ˣ
2 ¹⁰⁺	**5**	**4** ¹⁻	**1** ⁷⁺	**3**
1 ⁴⁻	**3**	**5**	**4**	**2**
5	**1** ²÷	**2**	**3** ¹⁻	**4**
4 ²⁻	**2**	**3** ⁹⁺	**5**	**1**

64

5 ¹²⁺	**1** ¹²ˣ	**4**	**3**	**2** ²÷
3	**2**	**5** ⁵	**1** ⁶⁺	**4**
2	**5** ⁸⁺	**3**	**4**	**1**
4 ¹⁻	**3**	**1** ²÷	**2** ¹⁵⁺	**5**
1 ⁵⁺	**4**	**2**	**5**	**3**

65

4 (11+)	2	5 (15×)	1	3
5	3 (9+)	4 (13+)	2 (2÷)	1
2 (2)	1	3	4	5 (1−)
1 (2−)	5	2	3 (30×)	4
3	4 (5+)	1	5	2

66

2 (30×)	5	3	1 (2÷)	4 (1−)
1 (2−)	4 (9+)	5	2	3
3	2 (1−)	4 (3−)	5 (6+)	1
5 (9+)	3	1	4 (2−)	2
4	1 (1−)	2	3 (2−)	5

67

3 (2−)	4 (1−)	5	1 (2÷)	2
1	2 (1−)	4 (1−)	3	5 (20×)
5 (5)	3	2 (2÷)	4	1
4 (2÷)	5 (9+)	1	2 (1−)	3
2	1	3	5 (1−)	4

68

1 (12×)	4	3 (9+)	5 (3−)	2
2 (6+)	3	5	1	4 (1−)
3	1	4 (2÷)	2	5
5 (3−)	2	1 (2÷)	4 (11+)	3
4 (1−)	5	2	3	1

69

5 (4−)	1	2 (1−)	3	4 (3−)
3 (6×)	2	4 (1−)	5	1
4 (7+)	3 (2−)	1 (2÷)	2	5 (3−)
1	5	3 (1−)	4	2
2	4 (1−)	5	1 (2−)	3

70

1 (2÷)	2	4 (20×)	5	3 (9+)
5 (4−)	1	3 (1−)	2	4
4 (14+)	5	2	3 (2−)	1
2	3 (2−)	1	4 (20×)	5
3	4	5 (1−)	1	2 (2)

71

3 (8+)	2 (2÷)	1	4 (11+)	5
4	1 (15×)	5	3	2
1	3 (60×)	2 (2)	5 (20×)	4 (7+)
2 (3−)	5	4	1	3
5	4	3 (6+)	2	1

72

4 (100×)	5	1 (2−)	3	2 (2÷)
5	3 (1−)	4 (2−)	2	1
1 (2÷)	4	2 (14+)	5	3
2	1 (2−)	3	4	5 (1−)
3 (1−)	2	5 (4−)	1	4

73

6× 3	2	3− 1	4	10+ 5
1− 5	1	1− 2	3	4
4	60× 3	5	2÷ 2	1
1− 2	60× 5	4	1	30× 3
1	4	3	5	2

74

1− 4	2− 3	2÷ 1	2	5 5
5	1	40× 2	2− 3	1− 4
3− 2	5	4	1	3
2− 3	2÷ 2	5	4 4	8+ 1
1	4	3 3	5	2

75

6× 1	2	2− 3	5	2÷ 4
3	8+ 1	1− 5	4	2
3− 2	3	4	9+ 1	5
5	8× 4	1	2	3
40× 4	5	2	2− 3	1

76

2− 2	4	11+ 3	8× 1	1− 5
7+ 1	3	5	2	4
5	1	2÷ 2	4	1− 3
1− 4	5	1	9+ 3	2
3 3	2− 2	4	5	1

77

40× 5	4	11+ 3	1− 1	2
3 3	2	5	5+ 4	1
2÷ 4	12× 3	1	2	2− 5
2	1	4	2− 5	3
8+ 1	5	2	3	4 4

78

96× 4	3	4− 5	1	8+ 2
2− 3	2	1− 4	5	1
1	4	3	40× 2	5
12+ 5	2÷ 1	2	4	1− 3
2	5	1	2− 3	4

79

11+ 2	1− 4	5	2− 1	3
5	1− 2	12× 4	3	8+ 1
4	3	20× 1	5	2
2− 3	4− 1	1− 2	4	5
1	5	3	2÷ 2	4

80

2÷ 2	4+ 3	1	1− 4	5
1	1− 5	1− 3	2 2	5+ 4
1− 5	4	2	2− 3	1
4	3− 2	5	1	1− 3
2− 3	1	20× 4	5	2

164

8/1

60× 4	5	3	2÷ 2	1
9+ 3	1	40× 4	5	2
5	8+ 3	2	3− 1	4
1	2	9+ 5	1− 4	3
2− 2	4	1	3	5 5

8/2

1− 5	4	4+ 1	1− 2	3
3− 1	2÷ 2	3	1− 4	40× 5
4	1	5 5	3	2
2− 3	5	2÷ 2	1	4
5+ 2	3	1− 4	5	1

8/3

7+ 2	60× 3	5	3− 1	4
1	4	1− 3	2	2− 5
4	2 2	10× 1	5	3
2− 3	10+ 5	2	12× 4	2÷ 1
5	1	4	3	2

8/4

60× 4	4− 5	1	7+ 2	1− 3
3	10+ 1	4	5	2
5	2	3	3− 4	1
2÷ 2	2− 3	5	1 1	20× 4
1	4 4	1− 2	3	5

8/5

1− 4	2÷ 2	6× 3	1	4− 5
5	4	2	8+ 3	1
3− 2	5	1	4	10+ 3
2− 1	1− 3	4	5	2
3	6+ 1	5	2− 2	4

8/6

3− 2	2− 3	8× 1	4	1− 5
5	1	2	4+ 3	4
1− 4	5	3 3	1	1− 2
2− 1	2 2	1− 4	5	3
3	4	5	2÷ 2	1

8/7

5 5	1− 3	2	6× 1	10+ 4
1− 4	5	3	2	1
2÷ 2	4	2− 1	3	5
5+ 1	3− 2	5	4 4	1− 3
3	1	1− 4	5	2

8/8

11+ 5	1	2÷ 2	12× 3	4
2	3	4	11+ 5	1
1 1	1− 4	6+ 3	2	5
1− 3	5	1	12+ 4	5+ 2
4	2	5	1	3

88/89

20×		3−		1−
1	**4**	**2**	**5**	**3**
2 2÷	**5**	**3** 7+	**1**	**4**
4	**3** 12+	**5** 12+	**2**	**1**
5	**1**	**4**	**3** 1−	**2** 10×
3	**2**	**1**	**4**	**5**

90

2−		6+		15×
4	**2**	**5**	**1**	**3**
2 2÷	**3** 60×	**4**	**5**	**1**
1	**5**	**3** 6+	**2** 2−	**4**
3 2−	**1**	**2**	**4** 24×	**5** 5
5 1−	**4**	**1**	**3**	**2**

91

3	3+		1−	2−	
3	**1**	**2**	**5**	**4**	**6**
1 8×	**2**	**5** 2−	**4**	**6** 3÷	**3** 3÷
5 3−	**4**	**3**	**6** 6	**2**	**1**
2	**6** 5−	**1**	**3** 2−	**5**	**4** 40×
6 2÷	**3**	**4** 2−	**2**	**1** 3÷	**5**
4 1−	**5**	**6** 5−	**1**	**3**	**2**

92

2−		2÷	90×		
6	**4**	**1**	**5**	**2**	**3**
4 1−	**6** 11+	**2**	**3**	**1** 5−	**5** 5
3	**5**	**4** 3−	**1**	**6**	**2** 3+
2 2÷	**3** 72×	**6**	**4**	**5** 90×	**1**
1	**2** 10×	**5**	**6**	**3**	**4** 2−
5 5	**1**	**3** 9+	**2**	**4**	**6**

93

1−		3÷	20×		12+
2	**3**	**1**	**4**	**5**	**6**
5 11+	**6**	**3**	**2** 3+	**1**	**4**
4 8×	**1**	**6** 11+	**5** 2−	**3**	**2**
6 5−	**2**	**5**	**1** 5+	**4**	**3** 3
1	**4** 12+	**2** 2÷	**3** 3−	**6** 3÷	**5** 6+
3	**5**	**4**	**6**	**2**	**1**

94

5	180×			5−	10+
5	**2**	**3**	**1**	**6**	**4**
3 3−	**5**	**6**	**2** 2÷	**4** 1−	**1**
6	**1** 5−	**2** 40×	**4**	**3**	**5**
2 2÷	**6**	**4**	**5**	**1** 2−	**3**
4	**3** 8+	**1** 4−	**6** 30×	**5**	**2** 4−
1	**4**	**5**	**3** 5+	**2**	**6**

95

3−	3÷		2−	10×	
4	**1**	**3**	**6**	**5**	**2**
1	**3** 2÷	**6** 3÷	**4**	**2** 2÷	**5** 1−
3 2÷	**6**	**2**	**5** 11+	**1**	**4**
6	**5** 40×	**4**	**2**	**3** 9×	**1**
2	**4**	**5** 13+	**1** 5−	**6**	**3**
5	**2**	**1**	**3** 1−	**4**	**6** 6

96

15×	2÷		7+	3−	
1	**4**	**2**	**5**	**3**	**6**
3	**6** 15+	**5**	**2**	**1** 5−	**4** 5+
5	**2** 10×	**4**	**3** 2÷	**6**	**1**
2 12+	**5**	**1** 5−	**6**	**4** 1−	**3** 3
4	**3** 3÷	**6**	**1** 1	**5**	**2** 3−
6	**1**	**3** 3	**4** 2−	**2**	**5**

97

10+ 4	30× 6	5	3÷ 2	3÷ 1	3
1	80× 5	4	6	1- 3	2
5	4	4+ 3	1	3÷ 2	6
8+ 6	3÷ 1	5+ 2	3	11+ 5	9+ 4
2	3	5- 1	80× 4	6	5
1- 3	2	6	5	4	1

98

6× 6	20× 4	5	1	1- 2	3
1	2÷ 6	3	1- 5	4	2- 2
2÷ 2	3+ 1	2÷ 6	3	15× 5	4
4	2	5- 1	6	3	11+ 5
13+ 5	3	10+ 4	2 2	1	6
3 3	5	2	4	5- 6	1

99

72× 6	4	3	3÷ 1	3- 5	3÷ 2
4 4	15× 5	1	3	2	6
2- 5	3	11+ 6	2- 2	3- 1	4
3	3+ 2	5	4	5- 6	1
12× 2	1	24× 4	6	11+ 3	5
1	6	7+ 2	5	4 4	3

100

5 5	1- 3	4	12× 2	5- 6	1
20× 4	5	6	1	5+ 3	2
2÷ 6	2÷ 1	2	1- 4	5	8+ 3
3	10+ 4	1	3÷ 6	2	5
3+ 1	2	5	1- 3	4	6 6
3÷ 2	6	15× 3	5	5+ 1	4

101

4 4	5- 1	2- 6	30× 2	3	5
3+ 2	6	4	4- 5	1	2÷ 3
1	4	1- 2	1- 3	10× 5	6
2÷ 3	5	5- 1	6	2	2÷ 4
6	3 3	15× 5	5+ 1	4	2
3- 5	2	3	4 4	5- 6	1

102

600× 5	3÷ 3	1	5- 6	2÷ 4	2
4	5	9+ 2	1	5- 6	1- 3
6	2	5	72× 3	1	4
2÷ 2	6 6	3	4	8+ 5	4- 1
1	4	5+ 6	15+ 2	3	5
3 3	1	4	5	3÷ 2	6

103

5+ 1	60× 5	3	4	3÷ 2	6
4	5- 6	1	6× 2	3	15× 5
1- 5	4	13+ 2	1	5- 6	3
2÷ 3	2 2	5	6	1	2÷ 4
6	1	3- 4	8+ 3	10+ 5	2
6× 2	3	6 6	5	4	1

104

5 5	2÷ 1	2	2÷ 3	6	24× 4
48× 4	11+ 5	6	3- 1	3	2
6	3- 2	5	4	20× 1	18× 3
2	2÷ 6	3	3- 5	4	1
7+ 1	3	15+ 4	2	5	6
3	4	1	6	3- 2	5

105

2−	2÷	11+	180×		2×
4	2	6	5	3	1
6	4	5	3	1	2
2− 5	**2÷** 1	2	4	**3−** 6	3
3	**1−** 5	**5−** 1	6	**2÷** 2	**9+** 4
2÷ 2	6	**3÷** 3	1	4	5
1	**24×** 3	4	2	**30×** 5	6

106

1−		4−		3÷	
5	4	6	2	3	1
4− 1	5	**1−** 3	4	**3÷** 6	2
3− 6	3	**9+** 5	**3+** 1	2	**72×** 4
3+ 2	1	4	**2−** 3	5	6
13+ 4	6	**10×** 2	5	**10+** 1	3
3	**2** 2	**5−** 1	6	4	5

107

2÷		5	18×		
4	2	5	6	1	3
3÷ 3	**90×** 6	**2÷** 4	2	5	**4−** 1
1	5	3	**3−** 4	**1−** 2	**11+** 6
1− 6	**8×** 4	2	1	3	5
5	1	**90×** 6	3	**2÷** 4	2
6+ 2	3	1	5	**2−** 6	4

108

16+		12×			3÷
6	5	3	4	1	2
5	**12×** 3	4	**3+** 1	**7+** 2	6
3− 3	6	1	2	5	**5+** 4
7+ 2	4	**11+** 5	6	**12+** 3	1
1	**2÷** 2	**16+** 6	3	4	5
4 4	1	2	5	**2÷** 6	3

109

3−		1−	6+	3÷	12×
2	5	4	1	3	6
1− 4	**24×** 6	3	5	1	2
5	4	**14+** 6	**7+** 3	2	1
3÷ 1	3	5	2	**6** 6	**20×** 4
3	**3+** 1	2	**10+** 6	4	5
4− 6	2	**3−** 1	4	**2−** 5	3

110

100×		10+	18×		6+
5	4	6	2	3	1
5− 1	5	4	3	**15+** 6	2
6	**1−** 1	2	4	5	3
144× 4	**2−** 3	1	**3÷** 6	2	**9+** 5
2	6	**15×** 3	5	1	4
3	**10×** 2	5	**1** 1	**2−** 4	6

111

2−	2÷		10×		
4	3	6	1	5	2
6	**2−** 4	**10+** 5	2	**3÷** 3	1
5 5	6	**8×** 1	3	**2−** 2	4
3÷ 1	2	4	**30×** 5	6	**14+** 3
3	**3+** 1	2	**96×** 6	4	5
10+ 2	5	3	4	**1** 1	6

112

10×	3+		2÷		1−
5	2	1	6	3	4
2	**10+** 4	**3−** 5	**6×** 1	6	3
1− 3	6	2	**150×** 5	**5+** 4	1
4	**9+** 5	**12×** 3	2	**5−** 1	6
5− 6	1	4	3	5	**20×** 2
1	3	**2−** 6	4	2	5

168

13

6 (5−)	1	3 (15×)	5 (11+)	4 (32×)	2
1 (8×)	2 (7+)	5	6	3 (3)	4
2	5	1 (3−)	4	6 (1−)	3 (3÷)
4	6 (3÷)	2	3 (36×)	5	1
3 (60×)	4	6	2	1 (30×)	5
5	3 (1−)	4	1 (3+)	2	6

14

6 (5−)	1	2 (24×)	3	4	5 (11+)
1 (3÷)	6 (10+)	5 (6+)	2 (5+)	3	4
3	4	1 (11+)	6	5 (6+)	2
2 (3−)	3 (9+)	4	5	1	6 (6)
5	2	3 (2÷)	4 (10+)	6	1 (3÷)
4 (9+)	5	6	1 (2÷)	2	3

15

2 (3÷)	6 (5−)	1	3 (60×)	4	5
6	2 (8+)	5	1	3 (3)	4 (10+)
3 (1−)	4	2 (2÷)	6 (11+)	5	1
1 (6+)	3 (3÷)	4	5	2 (4−)	6
5	1	3 (2÷)	4 (24×)	6	2 (1−)
4 (9+)	5	6	2 (3+)	1	3

16

5 (3−)	2	3 (3÷)	1	6 (24×)	4
3 (72×)	6	4	5 (4−)	1	2 (10×)
4 (3−)	1	6 (2÷)	3	2 (8+)	5
6 (12×)	3 (2−)	5	2	4	1 (1)
1	4 (2÷)	2	6 (11+)	5	3 (2÷)
2	5 (6+)	1	4 (1−)	3	6

17

2 (3−)	5	1 (2−)	3	4 (1−)	6 (6)
3 (2÷)	4 (24×)	6	1 (3+)	5	2 (7+)
6	3 (3)	4 (1−)	2	1 (6×)	5
1 (2÷)	2	3	5	6	4 (8+)
5 (20×)	6 (5−)	2 (2)	4	3 (1−)	1
4	1	5 (11+)	6	2	3

18

1 (12×)	4	3	5 (11+)	6	2 (3−)
3 (15×)	6 (5−)	4 (32×)	2 (6×)	1	5
5	1	2	4	3	6 (2÷)
2 (10+)	5 (11+)	6	1	4	3
6	2	1 (6+)	3 (3−)	5 (1−)	4
4 (7+)	3	5	6	2 (2÷)	1

19

4 (20×)	3 (3−)	2 (6×)	6 (11+)	5	1 (2÷)
5	6	3	4 (10+)	1	2
3 (15×)	5	6 (5−)	1	2	4 (9+)
6 (6)	1 (2÷)	4 (1−)	2 (5+)	3	5
1 (1−)	2	5	3	4 (10+)	6 (2÷)
2	4 (20×)	1	5	6	3

20

6 (11+)	2 (3÷)	3 (12×)	1	5 (40×)	4
5	6	4	3 (3÷)	1	2
3 (1−)	4	5 (60×)	6	2	1 (4−)
4 (2÷)	1 (5−)	6	2 (3−)	3 (12×)	5
2	3 (3÷)	1	5	4	6 (2÷)
1 (8+)	5	2 (24×)	4	6	3

1-2-1

3	4−		48×		
3	**5**	**1**	**6**	**2**	**4**
12+			5−		3+
4	**3**	**5**	**1**	**6**	**2**
36×			30×	3−	
2	**6**	**3**	**5**	**4**	**1**
11+	5+	2÷			2÷
5	**4**	**2**	**3**	**1**	**6**
				13+	
6	**1**	**4**	**2**	**5**	**3**
3+		2−			
1	**2**	**6**	**4**	**3**	**5**

1-2-2

5−		20×		6×	7+
6	**1**	**5**	**4**	**2**	**3**
3−	11+				
2	**5**	**6**	**1**	**3**	**4**
	8+			30×	2
5	**4**	**1**	**3**	**6**	**2**
1−	5+				5−
4	**3**	**2**	**5**	**1**	**6**
	2−		11+		
3	**2**	**4**	**6**	**5**	**1**
1	2÷		11+		
1	**6**	**3**	**2**	**4**	**5**

1-2-3

2÷	72×		3÷	3−	5−
2	**6**	**4**	**3**	**5**	**1**
	5				
4	**5**	**3**	**1**	**2**	**6**
16+			36×		
5	**4**	**1**	**6**	**3**	**2**
1−			3−		2−
3	**2**	**6**	**4**	**1**	**5**
5−	3+		3−	96×	
6	**1**	**2**	**5**	**4**	**3**
	2−				
1	**3**	**5**	**2**	**6**	**4**

1-2-4

3+		30×		12×	
1	**2**	**6**	**5**	**3**	**4**
24×		10×	1−		3÷
6	**4**	**5**	**3**	**2**	**1**
1−			10+		
5	**1**	**2**	**4**	**6**	**3**
	1−	9+	5−		13+
4	**5**	**3**	**6**	**1**	**2**
6×			40×		
3	**6**	**1**	**2**	**4**	**5**
	3				
2	**3**	**4**	**1**	**5**	**6**

1-2-5

3÷		1−	3	3−	
6	**2**	**5**	**3**	**1**	**4**
15×			5−	60×	3+
3	**5**	**6**	**1**	**4**	**2**
1−		2÷			
5	**4**	**2**	**6**	**3**	**1**
8+			9+		90×
1	**3**	**4**	**2**	**5**	**6**
	5−				
4	**6**	**1**	**5**	**2**	**3**
2÷		13+			
2	**1**	**3**	**4**	**6**	**5**

1-2-6

60×	5−		4	13+	2÷
3	**6**	**1**	**4**	**5**	**2**
		10+			
5	**4**	**3**	**6**	**2**	**1**
4			6×	3÷	11+
4	**5**	**2**	**3**	**1**	**6**
5−	2÷	2−			
6	**1**	**4**	**2**	**3**	**5**
			9+		1−
1	**2**	**6**	**5**	**4**	**3**
5+		4−		6	
2	**3**	**5**	**1**	**6**	**4**

1-2-7

24×	6	3−	4−	3−	
2	**6**	**3**	**5**	**1**	**4**
				8+	
3	**4**	**6**	**1**	**5**	**2**
5−	8+		2÷		
6	**3**	**5**	**2**	**4**	**1**
	2÷	9+		1−	
1	**2**	**4**	**3**	**6**	**5**
20×			1−		2÷
5	**1**	**2**	**4**	**3**	**6**
	6+		3÷		
4	**5**	**1**	**6**	**2**	**3**

1-2-8

2÷	1−	1−		5−	
4	**5**	**2**	**3**	**1**	**6**
		1−	4−		12×
2	**4**	**6**	**1**	**5**	**3**
12+	6×		4	2÷	
6	**2**	**5**	**4**	**3**	**1**
		3+			
5	**3**	**1**	**2**	**6**	**4**
	5−	7+	30×	2÷	
1	**6**	**3**	**5**	**4**	**2**
3				10×	
3	**1**	**4**	**6**	**2**	**5**

Puzzle 129

1− 4	600× 5	5− 1	6	3÷ 3	2÷ 2
3	6	5	2 2	1	4
11+ 5	4	36× 3	3+ 1	2	6 6
6	2÷ 1	2	12× 3	4	14+ 5
1− 1	2	6	120× 4	5	3
2	1− 3	4	5	6	1

Puzzle 130

2÷ 6	3	30× 1	9+ 5	4	2÷ 2
3+ 2	6 6	5	3÷ 3	1	4
1	25× 5	6	2÷ 4	5+ 2	3
5	1	9+ 4	2	2÷ 3	11+ 6
1− 3	4	2	5− 1	6	5
2÷ 4	2	3	6	4− 5	1

Puzzle 131

2÷ 3	6	120× 2	5	5+ 1	4
75× 5	3	4	4− 2	6	5− 1
2÷ 2	5	3	5+ 1	4	6
4	1	11+ 5	6	3− 2	5+ 3
48× 6	4	3÷ 1	3	5	2
1	2	6 6	12+ 4	3	5

Puzzle 132

8+ 1	3	2÷ 4	2	30× 5	6
11+ 5	4	5− 6	1	36× 3	3− 2
6	3+ 1	2	3	4	5
1− 3	1− 6	5	120× 4	3÷ 2	3÷ 1
4	10× 2	3÷ 1	5	6	3
2 2	5	3	6	5+ 1	4

Puzzle 133

12× 3	4	3+ 1	2	90× 6	5
2− 4	2	5	5− 6	1	3
3− 5	5+ 1	4	5+ 3	2	7+ 6
2	2÷ 3	6	4− 5	48× 4	1
6× 6	7+ 5	2	1	3	4
1	6 6	1− 3	4	3− 5	2

Puzzle 134

4− 5	4 4	2÷ 3	6	8× 1	24× 2
1	9+ 5	11+ 6	2	4	3
3÷ 6	3	5	3+ 1	2	4
2	1	7+ 4	2÷ 3	6	6+ 5
2÷ 3	6	2	1− 4	90× 5	1
2÷ 4	2	1	5	3	6

Puzzle 135

2− 6	15× 3	5	6+ 1	2÷ 4	2
4	6	5− 1	2	3	20× 5
30× 3	5	3÷ 2	5− 6	1	4
2	4	3− 6	8+ 3	5	5− 1
4− 5	1	24× 3	1− 4	3÷ 2	6
1	2	4	5	6	3 3

Puzzle 136

72× 3	4	10× 5	2	5− 1	6
6	2÷ 3	2 2	80× 4	4− 5	1
3− 2	6	1− 3	1	4	5
5	3+ 1	4	2÷ 3	6	2− 2
20× 1	2	5− 6	30× 5	18× 3	4
4	5	1	6	2	3

137

6	3	4	1	2	5
4	5	6	2	3	1
5	4	2	3	1	6
1	2	5	4	6	3
3	6	1	5	4	2
2	1	3	6	5	4

138

2	1	5	3	4	6
1	4	2	5	6	3
6	2	1	4	3	5
5	3	4	6	2	1
4	6	3	1	5	2
3	5	6	2	1	4

139

1	6	5	4	3	2
6	3	1	5	2	4
4	5	2	1	6	3
3	2	4	6	1	5
5	1	3	2	4	6
2	4	6	3	5	1

140

5	2	4	3	1	6
1	5	2	4	6	3
6	1	5	2	3	4
4	3	1	6	2	5
3	4	6	1	5	2
2	6	3	5	4	1

141

4	6	5	1	3	2
3	5	4	6	2	1
5	4	3	2	1	6
1	3	2	5	6	4
2	1	6	3	4	5
6	2	1	4	5	3

142

1	4	2	3	5	6
4	2	1	5	6	3
6	3	5	1	2	4
2	1	3	6	4	5
5	6	4	2	3	1
3	5	6	4	1	2

143

6	3	2	4	5	1
4	2	3	1	6	5
5	4	6	2	1	3
1	6	5	3	2	4
3	5	1	6	4	2
2	1	4	5	3	6

144

2	3	4	1	6	5
5	2	1	4	3	6
6	5	3	2	1	4
1	6	5	3	4	2
3	4	2	6	5	1
4	1	6	5	2	3

45× 3	5	2÷ 2	24× 6	4	1
5	3	4	2÷ 2	1	3÷ 6
15+ 4	6	5	3− 1	30× 3	2
5− 6	6+ 1	3	4	2	5
1	2	14+ 6	3	5	1− 4
7+ 2	4	1	11+ 5	6	3

30× 2	3	1	5	11+ 4	6
2÷ 3	1− 5	4	5− 6	1	3− 2
6	288× 4	3	1	6× 2	5
4	6	10× 5	1− 2	3	1
6+ 5	2÷ 1	2	3	90× 6	4 4
1	2	10+ 6	4	5	3

13+ 4	6	3÷ 1	3	50× 2	5
3	1 1	3÷ 2	6	5	2− 4
11+ 6	1− 4	5	3÷ 1	3	2
5	11+ 2	6	3− 4	1	3 3
2÷ 2	3	14+ 4	5 5	5− 6	1
1	5	3	2	2− 4	6

3+ 1	2	2÷ 3	6	24× 4	1− 5
100× 5	5− 1	6	3	2	4
4	5	3+ 1	2	2÷ 6	3
6 6	2− 3	5	3− 4	1	4− 2
1− 3	2÷ 4	2	1 1	15× 5	6
2	120× 6	4	5	3	1

2÷ 2	4	15× 3	5	5− 6	1
20× 4	3÷ 6	2	3	1	5
5	2÷ 3	6	3− 1	1− 4	3÷ 2
3+ 1	2	4− 5	4	3	6
2− 3	5	1	48× 6	2	4
5− 6	1	2÷ 4	2	2− 5	3

1− 5	6× 6	1	30× 2	3	72× 4
4	1	2	3+ 3	5	6
5− 6	2− 4	240× 5	1	3÷ 2	3
1	2	3	4	6	3− 5
5+ 3	5 5	4	1− 6	3− 1	2
2	2÷ 3	6	5	4	1 1

60× 6	2	3− 3	2÷ 4	6+ 1	5
11+ 4	5	6	2	3 3	3÷ 1
5	12× 1	2	6	1− 4	3
2	4	3− 1	8+ 3	5	72× 6
10+ 1	7+ 3	4	5	6	2
3	6	6+ 5	1	2÷ 2	4

10× 2	1	32× 4	14+ 3	5	7+ 6
5	4	2	6	1− 3	1
12+ 1	5	6	48× 4	2	2− 3
3÷ 6	2	3	1	4	5
72× 4	3÷ 3	1	12+ 5	5− 6	2− 2
3	6	5	2	1	4

153

```
3-   11+  1    12×  3÷
 4    5    1    3    6    2
          10×        1-   1-
 1    6    2    4    3    5
1-
 3    2    5    1    4    6
11+  11+            1-
 5    1    4    6    2    3
      1-   3-   3-        3-
 6    4    3    2    5    1
2         4-
 2    3    6    5    1    4
```

154

```
108×           4-        2÷
 6    3    1    5    4    2
2-        19+  9+   3÷
 4    6    5    2    1    3
                        40×
 2    5    3    1    6    4
3-             1-
 1    4    6    3    2    5
8+   3+             10+
 5    1    2    4    3    6
      2÷        1-
 3    2    4    6    5    1
```

155

```
2-   12+  2    10×  1-
 6    3    2    1    4    5
          5-        3-
 4    5    1    2    6    3
3+             60×  3÷
 1    4    6    5    3    2
      30×  36×
 2    1    3    4    5    6
                   7+
 5    6    4    3    2    1
6×        30×
 3    2    5    6    1    4
```

156

```
60×       11+       3÷
 3    1    5    4    2    6
          5-        72×
 4    5    2    1    6    3
3-        1-
 1    4    6    5    3    2
6+             13+
 2    3    1    6    5    4
540×                3-   6+
 5    6    3    2    4    1
      24×
 6    2    4    3    1    5
```

157

```
3-   12×  2÷        7+
 1    4    6    3    5    2
          2÷        11+
 4    3    1    2    6    5
2-   1    2÷        3-
 5    1    2    4    3    6
      150×      2÷        12×
 3    6    5    1    2    4
3÷        9+   5-
 2    5    4    6    1    3
                   1-
 6    2    3    5    4    1
```

158

```
11+  72×  3-        1-
 5    6    1    4    2    3
               13+  2÷
 6    4    3    5    1    2
3    1-                  16+
 3    5    4    2    6    1
96×            3÷
 4    2    6    1    3    5
      6+        3    1-
 2    1    5    3    4    6
3÷        3÷
 1    3    2    6    5    4
```

159

```
60×  12+  1    15×
 4    6    2    1    5    3
               3÷        2÷
 5    3    4    6    2    1
11+       60×  2÷
 1    4    6    5    3    2
3+                       20×
 2    1    3    4    6    5
2÷   3-   2-        11+
 6    2    5    3    1    4
                   2÷
 3    5    1    2    4    6
```

160

```
48×            13+  3    2÷
 6    4    2    5    3    1
4    5-
 4    6    1    3    5    2
6+   2÷   2-   2-        1-
 1    2    5    4    6    3
                   3÷
 5    1    3    6    2    4
2-        24×  2÷   5-
 3    5    4    2    1    6
1-                  1-
 2    3    6    1    4    5
```

161

2− **6**	**4**	2÷ **1**	7+ **2**	90× **3**	**5**
120× **4**	**1**	**2**	**5**	**6**	1− **3**
3÷ **3**	**5**	**6**	5− **1**	2 **2**	**4**
1	11+ **3**	**5**	**6**	2÷ **4**	**2**
3− **5**	**2**	**3**	5+ **4**	**1**	6 **6**
3÷ **2**	**6**	1− **4**	**3**	4− **5**	**1**

162

11+ **2**	5+ **4**	**1**	6× **3**	1− **5**	**6**
4	1− **3**	2− **6**	**2**	4− **1**	**5**
5	**2**	**4**	5− **1**	**6**	3 **3**
5− **1**	**6**	3− **2**	**5**	96× **3**	**4**
2÷ **3**	4− **1**	**5**	2− **6**	**4**	**2**
6	**5**	2− **3**	**4**	2÷ **2**	**1**

163

2− **4**	3÷ **1**	**3**	120× **6**	**5**	1− **2**
2	15+ **5**	8+ **1**	**4**	2÷ **6**	**3**
12+ **1**	**4**	**2**	**5**	**3**	6 **6**
5	**6**	12+ **4**	1− **3**	**2**	6+ **1**
6	**3**	**5**	2÷ **2**	**1**	**4**
36× **3**	**2**	**6**	**1**	1− **4**	**5**

164

24× **6**	**4**	2− **5**	**3**	1− **1**	**2**
16+ **5**	5− **6**	2÷ **1**	**2**	180× **3**	4 **4**
2	**1**	6 **6**	**4**	**5**	**3**
4	**5**	6+ **3**	**1**	**2**	15+ **6**
3÷ **1**	**3**	2÷ **2**	1− **6**	**4**	**5**
1− **3**	**2**	**4**	**5**	5− **6**	**1**

165

4− **1**	**5**	24× **6**	**4**	12+ **2**	**3**
2− **4**	**6**	9+ **1**	**2**	**3**	3− **5**
8+ **3**	3− **1**	5 **5**	**6**	**4**	**2**
5	**4**	6+ **2**	**3**	5− **1**	**6**
3÷ **6**	6× **2**	1− **3**	**1**	20× **5**	**4**
2	**3**	**4**	11+ **5**	**6**	**1**

166

5+ **4**	**1**	90× **5**	**3**	3÷ **6**	**2**
6+ **1**	3− **2**	480× **4**	**6**	**5**	2− **3**
2	**5**	**6**	**4**	3÷ **3**	30× **1**
3	2÷ **4**	**2**	**5**	**1**	**6**
1− **6**	13+ **3**	**1**	1− **2**	2− **4**	**5**
5	**6**	**3**	**1**	**2**	4 **4**

167

6× **6**	1− **5**	**4**	30× **2**	3÷ **1**	**3**
1	30× **6**	**5**	**3**	3÷ **2**	2÷ **4**
5+ **3**	7+ **4**	**1**	**5**	**6**	**2**
2	**3**	15+ **6**	**4**	**5**	30× **1**
11+ **4**	6+ **1**	**2**	5− **6**	**3**	**5**
5	**2**	**3**	1− **1**	**4**	**6**

168

3 **3**	1− **4**	5− **1**	11+ **5**	**6**	2÷ **2**
2÷ **2**	**5**	**6**	2− **4**	15× **3**	**1**
1	2÷ **6**	**3**	**2**	**5**	1− **4**
15+ **6**	2− **2**	**4**	2− **3**	**1**	**5**
4	3÷ **3**	60× **5**	**1**	4− **2**	**6**
5	**1**	**2**	**6**	1− **4**	**3**

169

3+ 1	**2−** 3	**2÷** 2	4	**1−** 6	5
2	5	**2÷** 3	6	**3−** 4	1
48× 3	4	**1−** 6	5	**1** 1	**3÷** 2
4	1	**5** 5	**1−** 3	2	6
1− 5	6	1	2	3	4
48× 6	2	4	**4−** 1	5	**3** 3

170

2− 4	2	**5−** 1	6	**180×** 5	3
2÷ 1	**20×** 5	**1−** 3	4	6	2
2	4	**2÷** 6	3	**16+** 1	5
11+ 5	6	**6+** 2	1	3	4
2÷ 3	**4−** 1	5	**2÷** 2	4	6
6	3	**1−** 4	5	**8+** 2	1

171

5− 6	1	**2÷** 2	5	**60×** 4	3
1− 5	4	1	**24×** 3	**8+** 6	2
2− 1	**2−** 5	3	4	2	**15+** 6
3	**3−** 2	5	**7+** 6	1	4
2÷ 2	**24×** 6	4	**9+** 1	3	5
4	**36×** 3	6	2	5	**1** 1

172

1− 3	4	**3÷** 2	6	**6+** 1	5
2÷ 2	**5−** 6	1	**20×** 4	5	**6×** 3
4	**2−** 5	3	1	**6** 6	2
6+ 5	**2÷** 1	**2−** 4	**11+** 3	2	6
1	2	6	**5** 5	**1−** 3	4
2÷ 6	3	**3−** 5	2	**3−** 4	1

173

3÷ 1	**30×** 6	**5+** 3	2	**1−** 4	5
3	5	1	**120×** 4	**3÷** 2	6
2÷ 4	2	5	6	**2−** 3	**12×** 1
13+ 2	**2÷** 3	6	1	5	4
6	**3−** 4	**10×** 2	5	**5−** 1	3
5	1	**1−** 4	3	6	**2** 2

174

3÷ 3	1	**2÷** 2	**120×** 4	**90×** 6	5
2÷ 1	2	4	6	5	3
10+ 2	5	**14+** 3	1	4	6
2− 4	3	**11+** 6	5	**2÷** 2	1
6	**24×** 4	**2−** 5	3	**6+** 1	**2−** 2
5 5	6	1	2	3	4

175

6× 6	1	**18+** 5	**1−** 2	**10+** 4	**1−** 3
20× 2	**5** 5	3	1	6	4
5	2	4	6	**10+** 3	1
3÷ 1	**1−** 3	2	**20×** 4	5	6
3	**15+** 4	6	5	**1−** 1	2
2− 4	6	**3÷** 1	3	**3−** 2	5

176

3− 1	**15+** 4	6	5	**6×** 3	2
4	**2÷** 2	1	**72×** 6	**30×** 5	3
5− 6	1	**2÷** 4	3	2	**1−** 5
2− 3	5	2	1	4	6
60× 5	6	**6×** 3	2	**5+** 1	4
2	**2−** 3	5	**2−** 4	6	**1** 1

176

177

Puzzle 177

60× 3	5	2− 6	4	2 2	4− 1
8× 2	4	10+ 3	5− 1	6	5
1	2− 3	5	48× 6	4	2
4	1	2	13+ 3	120× 5	6
1− 6	2÷ 2	1	5	3	4
5	2− 6	4	2	3÷ 1	3

Puzzle 178

3÷ 6	2	75× 5	8+ 3	4	1
3+ 2	5	3	60× 4	1	10+ 6
1	12× 3	10+ 2	6 6	5	4
4	1	6	2	3	2− 5
8+ 5	14+ 6	4	9+ 1	2	3
3	4	1	5	4− 6	2

Puzzle 179

4− 6	3÷ 1	3	60× 4	5	6+ 2
2	1− 5	6	3	12+ 4	1
1 1	2− 4	20× 5	6	2	3
90× 3	2	4	1	1− 6	5
5	6	8+ 1	2	3÷ 3	2− 4
9+ 4	3	2	5	1	6

Puzzle 180

36× 2	5− 6	1	12+ 4	3	5
6	3	10× 5	1	2	3− 4
2− 3	5	3÷ 2	6	1− 4	1
3− 1	4	2− 6	2 2	5	6× 3
6+ 5	1	4	2÷ 3	6	2
4 4	1− 2	3	30× 5	1	6

Puzzle 181

60× 3	24× 6	4− 5	1	36× 2	2÷ 4
5	4	1	6	3	2
4	2÷ 2	3− 6	3	6× 1	8+ 5
3+ 2	1	40× 4	5	6	3
1	2− 5	3	2	16+ 4	6
2÷ 6	3	2÷ 2	4	5	1

Puzzle 182

720× 6	2	4	5	3	1 1
15+ 4	5	36× 2	6	3÷ 1	3
5	1	3	72× 4	6	200× 2
2÷ 2	5− 6	1	3	5	4
1	216× 3	6	10× 2	12+ 4	5
3	4	5	1	2	6

Puzzle 183

40× 5	5− 1	2÷ 6	3	2÷ 2	4
4	6	3+ 1	2	2− 3	5
2	60× 5	3	5+ 1	4	5− 6
3	4	2	2− 6	1− 5	1
2÷ 1	2	5 5	4	6	6× 3
13+ 6	3	4	5 5	1	2

Puzzle 184

1− 2	1	72× 3	4	6	4− 5
10+ 4	5	3÷ 6	2	11+ 3	1
1	1− 4	5	6	2	2÷ 3
90× 3	6× 2	1	6+ 5	1− 4	6
6	3	48× 2	1	5	4 4
5	6	4	6+ 3	1	2

185

96× 4	15+ 6	1	2− 3	5	7+ 2
1	4	3	3÷ 2	6	5
6	9+ 1	5	2÷ 4	2	3− 3
2	3	2÷ 4	1− 5	4× 1	6
3	50× 5	2	6	4	1
5	2	10+ 6	1	3	4 4

186

5− 1	6	1− 3	4	2÷ 2	180× 5
2− 5	48× 4	2	6	1	3
3	10× 2	1	5	15+ 4	6
9+ 4	7+ 1	6	3÷ 3	5	2
2	3	20× 5	1	6	3− 4
1− 6	5	4	1− 2	3	1

187

30× 6	60× 3	5	4	1− 2	1
5	2÷ 4	2	1− 3	10+ 1	6
2÷ 1	4− 5	2÷ 6	2	15+ 4	3
2	1	3	5− 6	5	1− 4
12× 3	9+ 2	4 4	1	6	5
4	6	1	5 5	5+ 3	2

188

30× 2	3	5	20× 4	1	5− 6
1− 4	15+ 6	1− 2	5	18× 3	1
5	4	3	1	6	7+ 2
18× 1	5	12+ 4	6	2	3
3	2÷ 1	7+ 6	2	1− 5	4
6	2	1	3	4	5 5

189

4× 1	15+ 4	6	5	1− 3	2
4	1	2− 5	3	9+ 2	2÷ 6
7+ 2	1− 5	4	6	1	3
3	2	1 1	15+ 4	6	5
108× 6	3	2÷ 2	1	1− 5	4
5 5	6	1− 3	2	3− 4	1

190

1− 5	6	4	3÷ 1	3	8× 2
11+ 6	2	3	9+ 5	4	1
13+ 1	3	3+ 2	288× 6	13+ 5	4
3	5	1	4	2	6
4	4− 1	5	2	6	2− 3
2÷ 2	4	2÷ 6	3	1 1	5

191

72× 4	2÷ 6	3	3+ 2	1	5 5
6	3	3− 1	4	16+ 5	2
3− 2	5	13+ 4	5− 1	6	3
3÷ 3	1	2	18+ 5	4	6
6+ 1	2	5	6	10+ 3	4
5	2− 4	6	3	2	1

192

2− 6	1− 4	5	6× 2	3	6× 1
4	30× 5	2	3÷ 3	1	6
3+ 1	3	16+ 6	12+ 5	2	12+ 4
2	1	4	6	5	3
90× 3	2÷ 2	1	16+ 4	6	5
5	6	3÷ 3	1	4	2

178

193

14+ 5	6	3÷ 3	1	40× 2	4
12× 6	3	2÷ 1	2	12+ 4	5
2	5− 1	6	12+ 4	5	3
11+ 4	5	2	3	108× 6	1
1 1	2÷ 2	4	5	3	6
1− 3	4	30× 5	6	1	2 2

194

4× 4	1	11+ 3	5	19+ 6	2
1	2− 2	4	3	5	6
15+ 5	3	1	6	6× 2	4 4
2÷ 6	16+ 5	2÷ 2	4	1	3
3	6	5	7+ 2	4	9+ 1
48× 2	4	6	1	3	5

195

1− 6	5	3− 1	4	1− 2	3
30× 5	2÷ 2	4	1 1	2÷ 3	6
1	6	2− 3	5	2÷ 4	2
9+ 4	6+ 1	2	3	1− 6	20× 5
3	4 4	4− 6	2	5	1
2	8+ 3	5	5− 6	1	4

196

36× 3	5− 6	1	7+ 2	1− 4	5
4	3	2÷ 6	5	2 2	3− 1
4− 1	1− 2	3	2− 6	14+ 5	4
5	1	24× 2	4	3	6
1− 6	5	4	3	6× 1	2
40× 2	4	5	5− 1	6	3

197

8+ 2	4	2− 5	1	6× 6	3 3
15+ 4	2	3	10+ 5	5− 1	6
5	2÷ 6	2	3	10+ 4	1
6	3	24× 1	4	20× 2	5
2− 3	5+ 1	4	6	5	2
1	13+ 5	6	2	1− 3	4

198

3÷ 1	3	11+ 6	5	8× 2	4
4− 6	2÷ 4	2	8+ 3	5	1
2	1− 5	4	24× 6	1	36× 3
60× 3	30× 1	5	4	6	2
4	6	3+ 1	2	1− 3	30× 5
5	2 2	2− 3	1	4	6

199

2− 5	24× 4	1− 3	2	5− 6	1
3	6	1	2÷ 4	2	11+ 5
6× 2	3	11+ 5	8+ 1	4	6
11+ 4	2÷ 1	6	3	3− 5	2
6	2	1− 4	5	3÷ 1	1− 3
1	13+ 5	2	6	3	4

200

1− 4	12× 2	6	1	8+ 3	5
3	7+ 5	2	3÷ 6	20× 4	1
5− 1	2− 6	4	2	5	1− 3
6	1− 3	4− 1	7+ 5	2	4
8+ 2	4	5	36× 3	5− 1	6
5	1	3	4	4− 6	2

201

3÷ 6	1− 5	1− 2	3	3− 1	4
2	4	8+ 3	3− 1	30× 6	5
5− 1	6	5	4	3− 2	3÷ 3
7+ 4	3	11+ 6	13+ 2	5	1
6+ 5	1	4	6	3	2
1− 3	2	1	5	2− 4	6

202

20× 5	4	1	2÷ 6	3	2÷ 2
24× 3	11+ 6	2− 5	2÷ 2	1	4
2	5	3	24× 1	4	6
4	3÷ 1	3÷ 2	11+ 5	6	30× 3
1	3	6	1− 4	2	5
12+ 6	2	4	3	6+ 5	1

203

2÷ 2	1− 5	20× 1	4	2÷ 6	3
4	6	10+ 3	5	8+ 1	2
2− 3	2	5	5− 1	4	10+ 6
5	3÷ 1	16× 2	6	3	4
5− 6	3	4	2	10+ 5	4− 1
1	2− 4	6	3	2	5

204

12× 4	3	1	11+ 5	6	3− 2
3÷ 2	6	5+ 4	1	48× 3	5
2− 3	7+ 5	2	4	1	2÷ 6
5	5− 1	6	1− 2	4	3
5− 6	2− 4	2− 5	3	3− 2	5+ 1
1	2	3	6 6	5	4

205

5− 6	1	2÷ 2	20× 5	4	1− 3
1− 5	6	1	2	3	4
1− 3	3− 2	5+ 4	1	11+ 5	6
4	5	2÷ 6	3	2÷ 1	2
2÷ 2	1− 3	15+ 5	4	3÷ 6	6+ 1
1	4	3 3	6	2	5

206

3÷ 2	6	1− 3	20× 4	1	5
13+ 4	3	2	12+ 5	5− 6	1
6	3+ 1	4	3	15+ 5	1− 2
15× 1	2	11+ 5	6	4	3
3	20× 5	6	1− 1	2÷ 2	4
5	4	1	2	3− 3	6

207

2÷ 6	7+ 2	20× 4	5	7+ 1	9+ 3
3	5	2÷ 2	1	6	4
5− 1	6	1− 5	1− 3	4	2
3− 4	1	6	7+ 2	3	11+ 5
9+ 5	3	1	10+ 4	2	6
2 2	4	3	6	6+ 5	1

208

36× 2	6	4 4	3÷ 1	3	13+ 5
4− 5	3	3− 1	4	6	2
1	1− 4	3	13+ 2	5	6
3÷ 3	1	11+ 5	6	2÷ 2	3− 4
2− 6	120× 5	2	15× 3	4	1
4	2	6	5	3÷ 1	3

209

4 (1−)	3 (6+)	2	1	6 (30×)	5
5	2 (3÷)	6 (14+)	3	1	4 (4)
2 (6×)	6	1	4 (1−)	5 (3−)	3 (2÷)
3	1 (4×)	4	5	2	6
1	4	5 (1−)	6	3 (1−)	2
6 (1−)	5	3 (3)	2 (7+)	4	1

210

5 (4−)	3 (6+)	2	1	6 (2÷)	4 (1−)
1	4 (24×)	6 (3÷)	2	3	5
3 (1−)	6	4 (1−)	5	1 (1)	2 (36×)
4	1	5 (4−)	3 (1−)	2	6
6 (3÷)	2	1	4 (1−)	5	3
2 (2)	5 (15×)	3	6 (24×)	4	1

211

3 (2÷)	5 (15×)	1	6 (3÷)	4 (2÷)	2
6	3	4 (1−)	2	5 (4−)	1
1 (3−)	2 (3÷)	3	4 (10+)	6	5 (9+)
4	6	2 (3÷)	5 (2−)	1	3
5 (3−)	1 (3−)	6	3	2 (2)	4 (13+)
2	4	5 (4−)	1	3	6

212

3 (1−)	4	1 (2÷)	2	5 (30×)	6
1 (5+)	6 (15+)	4	5	2 (6×)	3
4	5 (11+)	6	3 (12+)	1 (2÷)	2
2 (3÷)	1 (2÷)	5 (2−)	6	3	4 (20×)
6	2	3 (24×)	1	4	5
5 (15×)	3	2 (2−)	4	6	1 (1)

213

2 (2÷)	5 (20×)	3 (11+)	6 (5−)	1	4 (7+)
1	4	6	2	5 (12+)	3
3 (3)	2 (9+)	5	1 (5+)	4	6 (12×)
5 (360×)	6	2	4	3	1
4	3	1 (3−)	5 (90×)	6	2
6 (5−)	1	4	3	2 (7+)	5

214

6 (6×)	1	2 (24×)	5	3 (2−)	4 (4)
1	3	4	6 (1−)	5	2 (48×)
5 (14+)	2 (6+)	1	3	4	6
4	5	3 (2÷)	2 (2÷)	6 (7+)	1
3 (9+)	4	6	1	2 (2÷)	5 (2−)
2	6 (120×)	5	4	1	3

215

4 (15+)	3 (2÷)	6	1 (12×)	2	5 (15×)
5	2 (2÷)	1 (20×)	6	4 (12×)	3
6	1	5	4	3	2 (12+)
3 (2−)	5	4 (2÷)	2	1	6
1 (13+)	6	2	3 (1−)	5 (2−)	4
2	4	3	5 (30×)	6	1

216

4 (2−)	1 (2÷)	2	6 (450×)	5	3
2	3 (3)	1 (13+)	4	6	5
1 (19+)	5	3	2	4 (12+)	6
5 (180×)	6	4	1 (6×)	3	2
6	4 (60×)	5	3	2	1 (6+)
3	2	6 (11+)	5	1	4

217

20×	360×			5−	
2	**4**	**3**	**5**	**1**	**6**
5	**2**	**6**	**4**(12×)	**3**	**1**(1)
3(1−)	**5**(8+)	**2**	**1**	**6**(2−)	**4**
4	**1**	**5**(1−)	**6**(2÷)	**2**(1−)	**3**
1(36×)	**6**	**4**	**3**	**5**(1−)	**2**(3−)
6	**3**(6+)	**1**	**2**	**4**	**5**

218

5−	54×		15+		
1	**3**	**6**	**5**	**4**	**2**
6	**2**(15+)	**3**	**4**	**5**(13+)	**1**
5	**6**	**2**(8×)	**1**	**3**	**4**
2	**4**(4)	**1**	**3**(1−)	**6**(12+)	**5**
3(12×)	**5**(11+)	**4**	**2**	**1**	**6**(2÷)
4	**1**	**5**	**6**(3÷)	**2**	**3**

219

15+	20×		3−		3÷
6	**4**	**1**	**5**	**2**	**3**
4	**6**(5−)	**5**	**2**(8+)	**3**	**1**
5	**1**	**6**(3÷)	**3**	**4**(3−)	**2**(11+)
3(30×)	**5**	**2**	**6**(11+)	**1**	**4**
1	**2**	**3**(1−)	**4**	**6**(180×)	**5**
2(5+)	**3**	**4**	**1**	**5**	**6**

220

120×				1−	
4	**5**	**1**	**6**	**3**	**2**
3(3)	**4**(7+)	**2**	**5**(30×)	**6**	**1**
6(1−)	**1**	**3**(1−)	**2**	**5**(8+)	**4**(15+)
5	**3**(6×)	**4**(2−)	**1**	**2**	**6**
1	**2**	**6**	**3**(7+)	**4**	**5**
2(3÷)	**6**	**5**(1−)	**4**	**1**(3÷)	**3**

221

1−	48×	5−		8+	
4	**2**	**1**	**6**	**5**	**3**
3	**4**	**2**(2−)	**1**(4−)	**6**(60×)	**5**
1(15×)	**6**	**4**	**5**	**3**(48×)	**2**
5	**3**	**6**(2÷)	**4**	**2**	**1**(6+)
6(3÷)	**5**(4−)	**3**	**2**	**1**	**4**
2	**1**	**5**(2−)	**3**	**4**(2−)	**6**

222

5+		3−	2−		2÷
1	**4**	**6**	**5**	**3**	**2**
2(3÷)	**1**(4−)	**3**	**6**(6)	**5**(1−)	**4**
6	**5**	**2**(10×)	**1**(3−)	**4**	**3**(3÷)
3(2÷)	**6**	**5**	**4**	**2**(15+)	**1**
4(1−)	**3**	**1**	**2**	**6**	**5**
5(14+)	**2**	**4**	**3**	**1**(5−)	**6**

223

2−		3÷	3÷	2−	
5	**3**	**2**	**1**	**6**	**4**
4(11+)	**1**	**6**	**3**	**5**(20×)	**2**(2)
6	**5**(8+)	**3**	**2**(11+)	**4**	**1**
2(2)	**4**(5+)	**1**	**5**	**3**(2÷)	**6**
1(5−)	**6**	**5**	**4**	**2**(1−)	**3**
3(9+)	**2**	**4**	**6**(12+)	**1**	**5**

224

5−		20×		2−	2÷
1	**6**	**4**	**5**	**3**	**2**
5(1−)	**2**(1−)	**3**	**6**(3÷)	**1**	**4**
4	**3**(2−)	**5**	**2**	**6**(5−)	**1**
6(2÷)	**4**(2÷)	**2**	**1**(3−)	**5**	**3**(8+)
3	**5**(6+)	**1**	**4**	**2**(3÷)	**6**
2(2)	**1**(7+)	**6**	**3**(12+)	**4**	**5**

225

[3−] 5	[2÷] 6	3	[1−] 4	[3−] 1	[1−] 2
2	[24×] 1	[3÷] 6	5	4	3
6	4	2	[3÷] 1	3	[11+] 5
[8+] 3	[2] 2	[2−] 4	6	5	1
1	[2−] 3	[3−] 5	2	[2−] 6	4
4	5	[2−] 1	3	[3÷] 2	6

226

[3÷] 6	[20×] 5	1	[2÷] 4	2	[3÷] 3
2	4	[36×] 6	[14+] 5	3	1
[8+] 4	[4−] 6	2	3	1	5
3	2	[4−] 5	1	[2−] 6	4
1	[15×] 3	[2÷] 4	2	[30×] 5	6
5	1	[72×] 3	6	4	[2] 2

227

[6+] 1	5	[6] 6	[1−] 3	4	[3−] 2
[1−] 3	4	[6×] 1	6	[2÷] 2	5
[9+] 5	[4−] 6	2	[2−] 4	1	[3÷] 3
4	[24×] 3	[15×] 5	2	[30×] 6	1
[3÷] 6	2	3	1	5	[2−] 4
2	1	4	[8+] 5	3	6

228

[72×] 6	4	3	[120×] 5	1	[24×] 2
[1−] 4	[4−] 5	1	2	6	3
5	[3] 3	[21+] 6	1	2	4
[7+] 1	[2÷] 2	4	3	5	6
2	[15+] 6	5	4	[9+] 3	1
3	1	[48×] 2	6	4	5

229

[3−] 5	[24×] 4	[1] 1	[1−] 3	2	[5−] 6
2	6	[18+] 5	[1−] 4	3	1
6	3	4	[5] 5	1	[1−] 2
[12×] 3	[1−] 1	2	[3÷] 6	4	5
1	[2−] 5	3	2	[12+] 6	[1−] 4
4	[3÷] 2	6	1	5	3

230

[1−] 3	4	[120×] 2	6	5	[17+] 1
[5−] 1	6	[9×] 3	2	4	5
[9+] 4	5	1	3	6	[3÷] 2
[16+] 2	3	[1−] 5	4	1	6
5	[13+] 2	6	[3÷] 1	3	[24×] 4
6	1	4	[5] 5	2	3

231

[2÷] 3	[5−] 1	6	[2÷] 2	4	[30×] 5
6	[1−] 4	5	[8+] 1	2	3
[10+] 4	6	[3] 3	5	[16+] 1	2
[3−] 2	[1−] 3	[3−] 1	6	5	4
5	2	4	[2÷] 3	6	[5−] 1
[8+] 1	5	2	[1−] 4	3	6

232

[30×] 5	6	1	[2÷] 4	[3÷] 3	[5+] 2
[13+] 4	5	[15+] 6	2	1	3
[9+] 2	4	3	6	[14+] 5	[1] 1
6	[6+] 1	2	3	4	5
1	[12+] 3	4	5	[12+] 2	6
[1−] 3	2	[30×] 5	1	6	4

233

3÷ 6	15+ 4	3− 2	5	2− 1	3
2	5	12× 6	1	7+ 3	4
10+ 4	6	3	2	4− 5	1
5	1	1− 4	3	2− 6	3− 2
3÷ 3	2÷ 2	1	6	4	5
1	3	1− 5	4	3÷ 2	6

234

10× 2	4	13+ 3	6	4− 5	1
5	3÷ 2	6	4	3÷ 1	3
7+ 4	15+ 6	5	1	3	18+ 2
3	9+ 5	2÷ 1	10× 2	4	6
5− 1	3	2	5	6	9+ 4
6	1	24× 4	3	2	5

235

1− 2	3− 3	12× 1	11+ 4	5	15+ 6
3	6	4	2	12× 1	5
6+ 1	5	3	6	2	4
30× 6	1	10× 2	5	1− 4	3
5	24× 4	6	3÷ 1	3	2÷ 2
40× 4	2	5	3	3− 6	1

236

12+ 3	6	8× 4	2	1	6+ 5
2÷ 2	3	15+ 5	4	6	1
1	2− 5	3	6	9+ 2	4
1− 6	1− 1	2	5	4	3
5	11+ 4	6	3÷ 1	1− 3	2
2− 4	2	1	3	5	6

237

2− 4	2÷ 3	6	1− 5	10× 1	2
6	9+ 2	3	4	5	1
9+ 1	12× 6	4	1− 2	3	15+ 5
5	1	2	2÷ 3	6	4
3	11+ 4	10× 5	1	2	6
2	5	5− 1	6	1− 4	3

238

32× 4	2	3÷ 6	8+ 5	3	4− 1
2− 3	4	2	5− 6	1	5
7+ 5	6	1	80× 2	4	1− 3
2÷ 6	3	20× 5	1	2	4
2÷ 2	6+ 1	7+ 3	4	5	3÷ 6
1	5	4	3− 3	6	2

239

8× 4	15+ 5	1− 2	18× 3	1	6
2	4	3	13+ 5	6	8+ 1
1	6	30× 5	2	4	3
12+ 3	1	6	1− 4	5	11+ 2
6	3	3− 4	1	2 2	5
5 5	2÷ 2	1	2÷ 6	3	4

240

1 1	30× 2	5	3	2− 6	4
2− 6	1− 4	3	4− 5	1	10+ 2
4	5− 6	2÷ 1	2	5	3
2− 3	1	4 4	7+ 6	7+ 2	5
5	5+ 3	2	1	1− 4	5− 6
3− 2	5	2− 6	4	3	1

241

6 (2÷)	5 (30×)	2 (7+)	4	1	3 (1−)
3	6	1	2 (2÷)	5 (15+)	4
5 (3−)	3 (2÷)	6	1	4	2 (2÷)
2	4 (1−)	3	5 (1−)	6	1
1 (1−)	2	4 (13+)	6	3 (1−)	5 (1−)
4 (4)	1	5	3	2	6

242

3 (2−)	1	6 (5−)	2 (3−)	5	4 (15+)
1	2 (60×)	4 (12×)	3	6	5
2	5	3	1 (5+)	4	6 (12×)
4 (17+)	3	5 (1−)	6	2	1
6	4	1 (2÷)	5 (1−)	3	2
5 (1−)	6	2	4	1 (3÷)	3

243

5 (5)	6 (4−)	2	1 (12×)	4	3
1 (3−)	4 (9+)	6 (15+)	3	2 (3−)	5
4	5	1 (3÷)	6	3 (15+)	2
6 (3÷)	2	3	5 (13+)	1	4
3 (6+)	1	4 (4)	2	5	6
2	3 (8+)	5	4 (24×)	6	1 (1)

244

1 (1)	3 (72×)	2	4	6 (12+)	5
4 (1−)	5 (15+)	3	6 (18×)	1	2 (2÷)
5	6	1	3	2 (10+)	4
2 (3÷)	4	6 (6)	5	3	1 (9+)
6	1 (10+)	4	2 (1−)	5	3
3 (1−)	2	5	1	4 (2−)	6

245

5 (10×)	2	4 (11+)	6 (2÷)	1 (3÷)	3
4 (120×)	5	2	3	6 (6×)	1
1 (4+)	6	5	2 (1−)	3	4 (15+)
2	1	3 (12+)	5	4 (2÷)	6
6 (13+)	3	1	4	2	5
3	4 (2−)	6 (8+)	1	5	2

246

6 (36×)	1 (8+)	5	2	4 (180×)	3
2	6 (5−)	1	3	5	4 (20×)
3	4 (12+)	2 (3÷)	6 (15+)	1	5
5	3	6	4	2 (2÷)	1
1 (10×)	2	4 (8+)	5	3 (2÷)	6
4 (4)	5	3	1	6 (3÷)	2

247

2 (2)	5 (40×)	4	1	3 (3−)	6
5 (20×)	2	1 (5−)	4 (2−)	6	3 (8+)
1	4 (13+)	6	3 (6×)	2	5
4	6	3	5 (10×)	1	2
3 (2÷)	1 (12×)	2	6	5 (80×)	4
6	3 (30×)	5	2	4	1

248

2 (48×)	6 (5−)	1	4 (1−)	3 (30×)	5
6	3 (12+)	4	5	1 (5−)	2
4	5	2 (60×)	1 (1)	6	3 (3÷)
5 (30×)	2	6	3 (1−)	4	1
3	1 (6+)	5	6 (16+)	2 (2)	4 (2−)
1	4	3	2	5	6

249

40× 5	11+ 3	2	6	3− 4	1
2	4	1− 6	15× 5	3÷ 1	3
4− 6	2	5	1	3	2− 4
15× 1	5	3	24× 4	2	6
7+ 4	5− 6	1	3	1− 5	3− 2
3	1	2÷ 4	2	6	5

250

2÷ 2	4	1− 6	60× 5	3	5+ 1
11+ 6	2	5	4	1	3
3	6	2× 2	1	1− 5	4
15× 5	3	1	2÷ 2	4	360× 6
4− 1	5	1− 4	36× 3	6	2
3− 4	1	3	6	2	5

251

5+ 1	3− 5	24× 2	4	14+ 3	6
4	2	2÷ 6	3	5	6+ 1
72× 6	4	3	12+ 1	2÷ 2	5
30× 2	3	5	6	1	4 (4)
3	5− 1	9+ 4	5	15+ 6	2
5	6	2÷ 1	2	4	3

252

20× 1	5+ 4	15× 3	5	4− 2	24× 6
5	1	1− 2	3	6	4
4	2÷ 6	1− 1	2	4− 5	1− 3
2÷ 6	3	5	4	1	2
3	3÷ 2	6	11+ 1	4	9+ 5
3− 2	5	4 (4)	6	3	1

253

5− 6	1	60× 5	4	3	15+ 2
2÷ 1	2	11+ 4	1− 6	3− 5	3
24× 3	6	1	5	2	4
4	20× 5	2 (2)	3÷ 3	1	6
2	4	11+ 3	120× 1	6	5
15× 5	3	6	2	4	1 (1)

254

2÷ 2	1	15+ 4	5	6	12× 3
1− 5	6	2÷ 3	30× 2	1	4
1− 4	2÷ 2	6	3	5	6× 1
3	4	3− 5	12× 1	2	6
9+ 1	3	2	6	9+ 4	5 (5)
6	5	5+ 1	4	3	2

255

2− 4	3÷ 6	2	15+ 5	3÷ 3	1
6	3÷ 1	3	4	2÷ 2	3− 5
3÷ 3	40× 4	5	6	1	2
1	2	6 (6)	6+ 3	1− 5	4
3− 5	2− 3	1	2	2− 4	2÷ 6
2	5	3− 4	1	6	3

256

5− 6	1	14+ 2	1− 5	4	1− 3
3÷ 1	2	6	1− 3	5 (5)	4
3	24× 6	4	2	6+ 1	5
40× 5	4	2− 3	1	3÷ 2	6
2	2− 3	20× 5	4	5− 6	1
4	5	1 (1)	11+ 6	3	2

257

[24×]6	4	[16+]5	[1−]3	[2÷]2	1
1	5	6	2	[9+]4	3
[1−]5	[18×]3	1	[10+]4	6	2
4	6	[6+]2	1	3	[1−]5
[1−]2	[1−]1	[1−]3	[1−]6	[4−]5	4
3	2	4	5	1	[6]6

258

[90×]5	6	3	[2÷]2	4	[5+]1
[1−]4	5	[2]2	[13+]6	1	3
[1−]3	[3÷]1	[2−]6	5	2	[20×]4
2	3	4	[5−]1	6	5
[5−]6	[11+]4	[8+]1	3	[2−]5	[4−]2
1	2	5	4	3	6

259

[1−]5	[6+]3	1	2	[48×]6	4
4	6	[1−]3	5	[2÷]1	2
[1−]3	5	[2−]6	4	2	[3÷]1
2	[12+]1	5	6	4	3
[7+]6	[2]2	[5+]4	1	3	[11+]5
1	[2−]4	2	[2−]3	5	6

260

[3÷]2	6	[10×]5	1	[11+]4	3
[3−]6	3	1	2	[5]5	4
[3−]1	4	[3−]6	3	[10×]2	5
[15×]3	[3−]5	2	4	6	1
5	1	[1−]4	[2÷]6	3	[14+]2
[2−]4	2	3	5	1	6

261

[2÷]6	3	[40×]4	5	[2÷]1	2
[17+]4	5	[18×]6	2	[3÷]3	1
2	6	3	1	[1−]4	[90×]5
[2−]3	[7+]1	2	4	5	6
1	[11+]4	[6+]5	[3−]6	[3÷]2	3
5	2	1	3	6	[4]4

262

[2]2	[2÷]3	6	[20×]4	1	5
[4−]5	1	[1−]3	[2÷]2	4	[2−]6
[11+]6	5	2	[2−]1	3	4
[2−]4	6	[3÷]1	3	[60×]5	[1−]2
[6×]1	[1−]4	5	6	2	3
3	2	[1−]4	5	[5−]6	1

263

[3−]4	[2−]1	[150×]5	3	[12+]6	2
1	3	2	5	4	[2−]6
[3÷]6	[60×]5	3	[1−]1	2	4
2	4	[24×]1	6	[2−]5	3
[1−]5	6	4	[15+]2	3	[5×]1
[5+]3	2	6	4	1	5

264

[2−]5	3	[2÷]2	1	[24×]4	6
[2÷]2	1	[14+]3	6	5	[4]4
[2−]4	6	[6×]1	[60×]3	[3−]2	5
[2−]3	[7+]5	6	4	[9+]1	2
1	2	[13+]4	5	6	[3÷]3
[6]6	4	5	[1−]2	3	1

265

2 [4−]	6	4 [5+]	1	5 [2−]	3
5 [4−]	1	2 [1−]	3	4 [2−]	6
6 [6×]	4 [1−]	5 [5]	2 [5+]	3	1 [40×]
1	3	6 [2−]	4	2 [3÷]	5
3 [15+]	2 [2÷]	1	5 [1−]	6	4
4	5	3	6	1 [1]	2

266

3 [2÷]	6	2 [2÷]	4	1 [5−]	5 [6+]
2 [1−]	3	4 [18+]	5	6	1
6 [120×]	4	3	1	5	2 [12+]
5	1 [4−]	6 [11+]	3	2	4
4 [7+]	5	1 [9+]	2	3 [10+]	6
1	2	5 [5]	6	4	3

267

2 [2÷]	4	6 [5−]	1	5 [15×]	3
6 [7+]	1	2 [1−]	3	4 [10+]	5
4 [2−]	6	3 [2−]	5 [13+]	1	2 [2÷]
1 [15×]	3 [3]	5	6	2	4
3	5 [7+]	4 [7+]	2	6 [13+]	1 [5−]
5	2	1	4	3	6

268

1 [40×]	3 [1−]	2	5 [1−]	6	4 [4]
4	2	3 [2÷]	6	5 [4−]	1
5	6 [5−]	1	3 [30×]	4 [2÷]	2
6 [14+]	4	5	2	1 [2−]	3
3	1	6 [11+]	4	2 [6×]	5 [1−]
2 [2]	5 [1−]	4	1	3	6

269

2 [6×]	3 [2−]	1	5 [1−]	4	6 [13+]
3	5 [1−]	4	6 [2÷]	2	1
5 [5]	6 [4−]	2	3	1 [6×]	4
4 [3−]	1	5 [3−]	2	6	3 [5+]
6 [5−]	4 [2÷]	3 [3−]	1	5 [13+]	2
1	2	6	4	3	5

270

4 [3−]	1	2 [2÷]	5 [30×]	3 [2÷]	6
1 [12×]	2	4	6	5 [11+]	3 [6+]
6	4 [1−]	5 [11+]	3 [2−]	2	1
3 [2−]	5	6	1	4	2
5	6 [3−]	3	2 [8×]	1 [5−]	4 [1−]
2 [1−]	3	1	4	6	5

271

1 [120×]	6	4 [56×]	7	2	3 [90×]	5
5	4	3 [15×]	1	7 [6−]	6 [13+]	2
4 [48×]	2	6	5	1	7	3
2 [6×]	1 [15×]	5	3	6 [17+]	4 [2÷]	7 [17+]
3	7 [6−]	1	6	5	2	4
7 [1−]	5 [30×]	2	4 [56×]	3 [2−]	1	6
6	3	7	2	4 [4]	5 [4−]	1

272

4 [5+]	1	5 [1−]	7 [4−]	6 [30×]	2 [2÷]	3 [5+]
7 [84×]	6	4	3	5	1	2
3 [3÷]	2	6 [11+]	5	4 [3−]	7 [13+]	1 [6+]
1	3 [6×]	2	4 [2−]	7	6	5
2 [3÷]	7 [6−]	1	6	3 [1−]	5 [9+]	4 [17+]
6	5 [14+]	3 [4−]	1 [2÷]	2	4	7
5	4	7	2	1 [2−]	3	6

273

13+ 6	6− 1	7	1− 5	4	6× 2	3
7	13+ 2	5	24× 4	6	3÷ 3	1
7+ 4	3	6	5− 2	3÷ 1	5 5	14+ 7
3÷ 1	3÷ 6	2	7	3	120× 4	5
3	3− 7	4	5− 1	5	6	2
3− 2	60× 5	3	6	8+ 7	1	2− 4
5	4	3÷ 1	3	14× 2	7	6

274

1− 3	13+ 7	6	1− 4	5	2÷ 2	1
4	144× 3	5 5	6− 7	1	18× 6	3− 2
5− 7	4	2	6	3	1	5
2	6− 1	7	4− 5	1− 4	3	2÷ 6
11+ 5	6	14+ 4	1	4− 2	18+ 7	3
5− 1	5	3	2	6	4	7
6	2÷ 2	1	3 3	16+ 7	5	4

275

3÷ 6	140× 4	6− 1	7	12+ 3	10× 2	5
2	5	7	19+ 4	6	3	1
21× 7	1	3	6	5	4	24× 2
3+ 1	2	2− 5	3	13+ 7	6	4
60× 4	168× 6	7+ 2	5	8+ 1	7	3
3	7	4	2÷ 1	2 2	18+ 5	6
5	3− 3	6	2	5+ 4	1	7

276

1− 2	1470× 7	5	3− 6	3	10+ 1	10+ 4
3	2÷ 4	7	20× 5	14× 2	6	1
3− 1	2	6	4	7	3	5
4	1− 1	2	13+ 7	6	9+ 5	21× 3
14+ 6	3	3÷ 1	2÷ 2	140× 5	4	7
5	18+ 6	3	1	4	7	4− 2
7	5	12× 4	3	3+ 1	2	6

277

10+ 4	4− 1	5	24× 2	378× 3	7	6
6	25+ 5	7	4	1 1	8+ 2	3
3÷ 1	7	6	3	11+ 5	4	2
3	2÷ 4	2÷ 2	1	6	35× 5	7
35× 5	2	2÷ 3	6	6− 7	1	10+ 4
7	2− 6	4	10+ 5	2	3	1
2 2	11+ 3	1	7	10+ 4	6	5

278

30× 3	13+ 7	5	3+ 2	1	96× 4	6
2	5	1	11+ 6	1− 3	13+ 7	4
6+ 5	1	2	3	4	6	2− 7
6− 1	2÷ 2	3− 4	7	2÷ 6	3	5
7	4	6× 6	1	10+ 2	5	3
24× 4	6	60× 3	5	35× 7	5+ 2	1
2÷ 6	3	7 7	4	5	1	2

279

32× 2	4	105× 7	15+ 1	5	6	3
4	14+ 6	3	5	3+ 1	2	7 7
13+ 6	5	4− 1	10+ 4	10+ 7	3	3+ 2
7	3	5	6	2− 2	4	1
42× 3	7	2÷ 4	2	3− 6	4− 1	9+ 5
1	2	1− 6	7	3	5	4
6+ 5	1	1− 2	3	4 4	7	1− 6

280

3÷ 6	2	1− 3	4	2− 1	35× 5	7
2 2	6− 7	5− 6	1	3	60× 4	5
11+ 4	1	2	6	5− 5	11+ 7	12+ 3
1	3	7	5	13+ 6	3+ 2	24× 4
3	40× 4	5	2	7	1	6
23+ 5	6	5+ 1	18+ 7	1− 4	3	1− 2
7	5	4	3	2	6	1

281

1− 6	5	168× 4	7	10+ 1	2	1− 3
8+ 1	2÷ 2	6	16+ 5	12× 3	7	4
7	1	5	6	4	5+ 3	2
10× 2	2− 6	6+ 1	2− 3	5	12+ 4	7
5	4	3	15+ 2	7	6	1
4− 3	7	2	28× 4	6× 6	1	1− 5
7+ 4	3	7	1	10× 2	5	6

282

4− 1	140× 7	5	2− 4	2	5− 6	1− 3
5	4	126× 7	2÷ 3	6	1	2
6 6	6+ 2	3	3− 7	4	15+ 5	1
84× 3	1	6	3÷ 2	2− 5	7	4
4	3	1	6	5− 7	2	5
7	17+ 5	6+ 2	1	3	12× 4	1− 6
2	6	4	4− 5	1	3	7

283

14+ 6	4	11+ 3	60× 5	2	7	15+ 1
4	1	7	504× 3	6	2	5
6+ 3	1− 5	6	4	7	1	14× 2
2	2− 3	5	6− 1	1− 4	6	7
1	8+ 2	4	7	5	1− 3	2÷ 6
5 5	20+ 7	2	18× 6	1	4	3
7	6	2÷ 1	2	3	5	4

284

12× 1	4	3	22+ 7	16+ 2	5	6
1− 2	5	6	4	1	7	3
3	4− 1	5	504× 6	4	84× 2	7
24× 4	2	6− 1	3	7	6	8+ 5
210× 6	3	7	20× 1	5	4	2
5	3− 7	4	10+ 2	14+ 6	3	1
7	3÷ 6	2	5	3	1	4

285

21× 7	3	3+ 1	11+ 5	13+ 6	1− 4	3− 2
4 4	1	2	6	7	3	5
3÷ 6	14+ 4	30× 5	3	2	42× 7	1
2	7	3	4− 1	5	6	2− 4
9+ 3	2	4	22+ 7	10+ 1	5	6
1− 5	6	7	2	4	6+ 1	3
6+ 1	5	6	7+ 4	3	2	7

286

24× 4	6	3+ 2	1	2− 7	10× 5	1− 3
7 7	1− 3	120× 6	4	5	1	2
21× 1	4	5	3÷ 6	2÷ 3	2	12+ 7
3	7	11+ 1	2	6	17+ 4	5
1− 5	2 2	3	7	4	6	3− 1
6	6− 1	7	3− 5	2	3	4
3− 2	5	1− 4	3	1 1	1− 7	6

287

14+ 4	3	1− 5	6	2÷ 2	1	16+ 7
1	5 5	42× 6	7	2− 3	4	2
6	13+ 1	12× 4	10× 2	5	7	3
2	7	3	5	5+ 1	6	4 4
3	120× 2	12+ 7	1	4	15× 5	5− 6
5	6	2	4	42× 7	3	1
28× 7	4	3÷ 1	3	6	7+ 2	5

288

1− 6	4− 7	3	3− 4	1	3− 2	5
5	2÷ 6	1− 4	13+ 7	24× 2	3	2× 1
6− 7	3	5	6	4	1	2
1	60× 4	12+ 7	2	1− 6	90× 5	3
3	5	2	1	7	2− 4	6
2− 4	2÷ 2	5− 1	13+ 5	3 3	6	11+ 7
2	1	6	3	5	7 7	4

Puzzle 289

6 (13+)	5 (10×)	2	4 (11+)	3 (1−)	1 (6−)	7
3	1 (2÷)	6 (30×)	7	2	5 (2−)	4 (24×)
4	2	5	3 (16+)	1	7	6
1 (6−)	6 (3−)	3	5	7	4 (2÷)	2
7	4 (84×)	1 (3−)	2 (7+)	5	6 (3−)	3
2 (3−)	7	4	1 (7+)	6 (3−)	3	5 (6+)
5	3	7 (7)	6	4 (2÷)	2	1

Puzzle 290

5 (3−)	2	3 (84×)	4 (5+)	1	7 (13+)	6
6 (24×)	5 (12+)	4	7	2 (6×)	3 (3÷)	1
4	1	6	2 (10+)	3	5 (5)	7 (56×)
1 (3+)	6 (16+)	5	3	7 (11+)	2	4
2	3	7	6	4 (10+)	1	5
3 (84×)	7 (6−)	1	5	6	4	2 (36×)
7	4	2	1 (1−)	5	6	3

Puzzle 291

7 (210×)	6	5	3 (105×)	4 (7+)	1	2
2 (2÷)	3 (10+)	7	1	5	4 (10+)	6
4	1 (2−)	3	7	2 (60×)	6	5
1 (6+)	5 (280×)	2	6 (4−)	3 (10+)	7	4 (3−)
5	7	4	2	6 (126×)	3	1
3 (2÷)	4 (2÷)	6 (1−)	5	1	2 (3−)	7 (21×)
6	2	1 (3−)	4	7	5	3

Puzzle 292

4 (60×)	3	5	1 (3−)	7	2 (6−)	6 (60×)
3 (12+)	2	7	4	1	6 (2÷)	5
5 (12+)	1	4 (3−)	7	6	3 (4−)	2 (56×)
1 (2÷)	6	3 (15×)	5	2	4	7
2	4 (1−)	1	6 (2−)	5	7 (4−)	3
7 (20+)	5	6 (3÷)	2	3	1 (3−)	4
6	7	2 (1−)	3	4 (4)	5 (6+)	1

Puzzle 293

3 (24×)	4	2 (84×)	7	1 (1)	5 (11+)	6
1	2	4 (1−)	6	5 (20+)	3	7
6	1 (2−)	3	2 (56×)	4	7	5
2 (17+)	3	6 (18+)	5	7	4 (16×)	1
5	6	7 (4−)	3	2 (24×)	1	4
4	7 (35×)	5	1 (3−)	6	2	3 (6×)
7 (2−)	5	1	4	3 (2÷)	6	2

Puzzle 294

1 (8+)	7	2 (1−)	3	5 (50×)	6 (10+)	4
3 (7+)	6 (3÷)	5	2	1	4 (3−)	7
4	2	7 (19+)	5	6 (3÷)	3 (2−)	1 (5−)
5 (1−)	3 (7+)	4	7	2	1	6
6	1 (4−)	3 (2÷)	2 (140×)	4	7	5 (5+)
2 (13+)	5	6	1 (11+)	4	7 (3−)	3
7	4	1	6	3	2 (3−)	5

Puzzle 295

4 (2÷)	2	6 (5−)	1	3 (6+)	7 (105×)	5
5 (17+)	6	7 (140×)	4	2	3	1
6	7 (3−)	4	5	1	2 (11+)	3
2 (1−)	3	5 (14+)	7	4 (5+)	1	6
1	5 (2−)	3	2	7 (13+)	6 (10+)	4
7 (3−)	4	1 (3÷)	3	6	5 (7+)	2
3 (3)	1 (9+)	2	6	5 (140×)	4	7

Puzzle 296

2 (4−)	6	4 (12×)	7	1 (5−)	5 (15+)	3
5 (15×)	7 (14×)	3	2	6	4 (6+)	1
3	2	7 (35×)	5	4 (24×)	1	6 (1−)
4 (1−)	5	1 (3÷)	3	2	6 (3÷)	7
7 (18+)	4	6 (5−)	1	3	2	5 (16+)
1	3 (6+)	2	6 (2−)	5	7 (2−)	4
6	1	5 (5)	4	7	3 (1−)	2

297

4−5	1	2÷4	2	105×3	13+6	7
2÷4	2	10+1	5	7	3−3	6
105×1	7	3	6	2÷4	8+5	2
3	5	2−6	4	2	56×7	1
504×6	1−3	2−5	6−7	1	2	4
2	4	7	6×3	5−6	1	15×5
7	6	2	1	1−5	4	3

298

84×6	7	2	17+5	5+1	3	1−4
2÷4	36×2	6	7	5	1	3
2	7+4	3	14+6	210×7	5	1
6+5	3	210×7	1	6	2−4	2
1	6	5	4	3	5−2	7
8+7	1	8×4	1−3	2	168×6	1−5
15×3	5	1	2	4	7	6

299

12×2	6	1	2−7	5	2÷3	16+4
12+7	2	3−5	3÷3	4	6	1
13+4	3	2	1	35×7	5	6
3	4	3−7	14+6	1	2	5
6	6−7	4	5	6×3	1	2
6+5	1	6×3	2	168×6	4	4−7
1	1−5	6	2÷4	2	7	3

300

36×3	3−7	4	1−5	6	2÷1	2
2	5×5	3−6	3	6+1	3−7	8+4
6	10+2	7	1	5	4	3
1−4	3	9+2	84×6	7	5×5	1
6+5	1	3	4	2	4−6	7
8+1	1−4	5	12+7	3	2	6
7	5−6	1	2	12+4	3	5